# Bladesmithing for Beginners + Bladesmithing from Scrap Metal + Heat Treatment Secrets

# TABLE OF CONTENTS

# Book 1: Bladesmithing for Beginners

# Book 2: Bladesmithing from Scrap Metal

# Book 3: Heat Treatment Secrets for Bladesmithing

# Bladesmithing for Beginners

*Make Your First Knife in 7 Steps*

# Introduction

One of the earliest knives made from smelted metal was discovered in a tomb in Anatolia. It was dated to the year 2,500 BC. However, iron was not included as a vital material in the making of knives until the year 500 BC.

Since then, the metal took new importance in crafting of various tools and implements. Greeks, Celts, Egyptians, and Vikings began to use iron into their metalworks. It was not until the development and discovery of steel that metalwork took on a whole new form.

We have come a long way since the first time man discovered the use of iron. Back then, the tools and knives that were produced were crude implements. They were there to serve a necessity and made using simple techniques.

Today, knife making is a process. It starts with finding the right steel, forging the knife, then subjecting the tool to an annealing and normalizing process. It is then shaped with grinding, heat treated, quenched, and finally tempered.

While our ancestors may not have been particularly careful about their working conditions, we should always make sure that we protect ourselves.

- Implement the use of safety glasses to protect our eyes from unwanted materials - such as hot metal and sharp debris - from flying into our eyes.
- Hearing protection is vital since prolonged exposure to loud sounds (for example, the noise of metal grinding) can affect hearing.
- Use a respirator to protect from tiny dust and other particles that can enter the lungs and cause permanent damage.
- Do not wear shorts, even on hot days. Hot sparks can fly off the metal and burn the skin.
- Put on leather bibs so that any stray spark hits a layer of fireproof material rather than your clothes.
- Tie up long hair when working with tools and metals. Make sure to secure a longer beard or keep them away using other means during metalworking.
- Since you are just starting, get comfortable using gloves. Eventually, they can become optional as you gain experience working with metals. But for now, better to err on the side of caution. Note: Do not use gloves while using any sort of spinning tool like a buffer or grinder. They could get caught in the mechanism.

Most importantly, have fun in the process. Don't be afraid to experiment. After all, it is only through experimentation that you can find out what you should do and what you are not supposed to do. Familiarize yourself with the basics and put the things you learn into practice.

Mistakes happen. That's alright. You may find out that your knives break, or you have an oddly shaped knife in your hands. Remember, there are only two things that are going to happen during knife making:

- You make a knife, whether it is perfect or not.
- You learn a lesson.

The lessons you learn are one of the most important aspects of knife making. You go from making regular knives to creating something like the one below.

Figure 1: Knife with tasteful curves.

So do not easily despair when you are working on your knife. Keep your focus on what you want to achieve, and you will get there eventually.

Take your time to understand the steps and information provided in this book. Make sure you know what you are working with and keep trying until you perfect it.

Design, Stock removal, grinding bevels, heat treatment, adding the handle, polishing, sharpening – these are the 7 steps with which you will make your first knife. But it's not the what, but the how to that will make you learn this craft.

With that, let's dive deeper into the art of bladesmithing.

# Free Bonuses for the Readers

First of all, I want to congratulate you on taking the right steps to learn and improve your bladesmithing skills, by buying this book.

Few people take action on improving their craft, and you are one of them.

This book has exhaustive knowledge on bladesmithing and will help you make your first knife.

However, to get the most out of this book, I have 3 resources for you that will REALLY kickstart your knife making process and improve the quality of your knives.

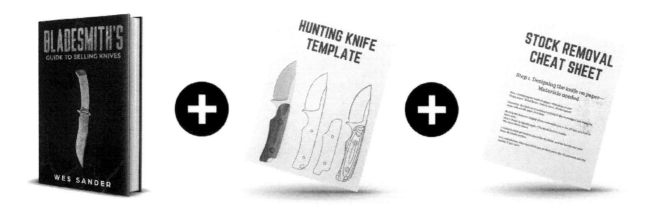

Since you are now a reader of my books, I want to extend a hand, and improve our author-reader relationship, by offering you all 3 of these bonuses for FREE.

Go to https://www.forge-hero.com/free-bonus and enter the e-mail where you want to receive these resources.

These bonuses will help you:

1. Make more money when selling your knives to customers

2. Save time while knife making

**Here's what you receive for FREE:**

1. Bladesmith's Guide to Selling Knives
2. Hunting Knife Template
3. Stock Removal Cheat Sheet

Here is a brief description of what you will receive in your inbox:

## 1. Bladesmith's Guide to Selling Knives

Do you want to sell your knives to support your hobby, but don't know where to start?

Are you afraid to charge more for your knives?

Do you constantly get low-balled on the price of your knives?

*'Bladesmith's Guide to Selling Knives'* contains simple but fundamental secrets to selling your knives for profit.

Both audio and PDF versions are included.

**Inside this book you will discover:**

- How to **make more money** when selling knives and swords to customers (Higher prices)

- The **hidden-in-plain-sight** location that is perfect for selling knives (Gun shows)

- Your **biggest 'asset'** that you can leverage to charge higher prices for your knives, and **make an extra $50 or more** off of selling the same knife.

- 4 critical mistakes you could be making, that are **holding you back from selling your knife for what it's truly worth**

- The ideal number of knives you should bring to a knife show

- 5 online platforms where you can sell your knives

- 9 key details you need to mention when selling your knives online, that will increase the customers you get

**2. Hunting Knife Template for Stock Removal**

Tired of drawing plans when making a knife?

Not good at CAD or any sort of design software?

Make planning and drawing layouts a 5-second affair, by downloading this classic bowie knife design that you can print and grind on your preferred size of stock steel.

**Here's what you get:**

- Classic bowie knife design **you can print and paste** on stock steel and start grinding

- Remove the hassle of planning and drawing the knife layout during knife making

- Detailed plans included, <u>to ensure straight and clean grind lines</u>

## 3. Stock Removal Cheat Sheet

Do you need to quickly lookup the correct knife making steps, while working on a knife in your workshop?

**Here's what you get:**

- Make your knife through stock removal in just **14 steps**

- <u>Full stock removal process</u>, done with 1084 steel

- **Quick reference guide** you can print and place in your workshop

As mentioned above, **to get access to this content, go to** *https://www.forge-hero.com/free-bonus* **and enter the e-mail where you want to receive these 3 resources.**

**DISCLAIMER:** By signing up for the free content you are also agreeing to be added to my bladesmithing e-mail list, to which I send helpful bladesmithing tips and promotional offers.

I would suggest you download these resources before you proceed further, as they are a great supplement for this book, and have the potential to bring an improvement in your results.

# Chapter 1: Tools of the Trade

This book has been designed to include as little filler material as possible. This allows you to jump into a process and start working on it immediately. One way to approach this book is to read a chapter then apply it in your workshop. Try practicing and understanding the techniques in each section before you move on to the next one. This will allow you to absorb the information better and memorize one technique before you begin with the next.

But before you even begin working on metals, you do need to know all the essential tools for the process.

## Tools for Your Workspace

The process of knifemaking is more than just about applying skills to create something. As you continue to make progress in knifemaking, you will be using various tools to get the results that you want. You need one set of tools to get the shape of the knife and another to make its surface smooth. The following tools will act as a starting point for making your first knife based on the processes mentioned in this book. As you get familiar with the process, I encourage you to experiment and improvise with the tools to find a technique that works best for you.

## Workbench

Your workbench is going to be your main space for a lot of your work. But more than that, it will act as a space to host all the vital tools you require. One of the essential things to note is that your workbench should be elevated to a comfortable height. By doing so, you won't have to bend over and strain your back muscles while working. Additionally, it's very important that your workbench be stable so that it doesn't move around when you're working on your blade. If anchoring it to the floor or wall isn't possible, try to add weight on the bottom to create a solid base with as little movement as possible.

## Angle Grinder

It is not necessary to have this tool right way. However, it definitely saves time when using it for different tasks such as grinding or cutting metal. An important point to note here is that you need to be extremely cautious when handling an angle grinder.

## Drill

Since you will need a tool that can easily punch holes into the knife's tang (more on this later) so that you can attach your handle, it is important to get yourself a drill press. You can also make use of a hand drill, but a drill press allows you to make accurate holes while you balance your knife carefully.

## Files

While the bulk of the work is done using power tools, it is nonetheless useful to have a file around. You can accomplish specific tasks efficiently, such as quickly removing a minor metal burr or fine-tuning the knife design. When you have a file around, you can take your time to work on your knife and get the result that you want.

## Belt Grinder/Belt Sander

A valuable tool to have in your work space, and as you will notice when we start working with knives, it is an essential part of the process.

You can always use the angle grinder to perform many of the tasks of a belt grinder, but I would recommend keeping the angle grinder for cutting. The belt grinder is much safer and easier to use. Plus, you can perform a plethora of tasks on it including shaping handles, grinding bevels, adding the finishing touches to your knife, and more.

One of the cheaper options for a belt grinder is the 1 x 30-inch version. The grinder itself won't be as rugged or versatile as the other varieties that you can get in the market, but it will help you out as a beginner.

The more expensive version is the 2 x 72-inch belt grinder. With the step-up in investment, you also get a hardier and sturdier grinder. This will improve the quality of the output you are producing.

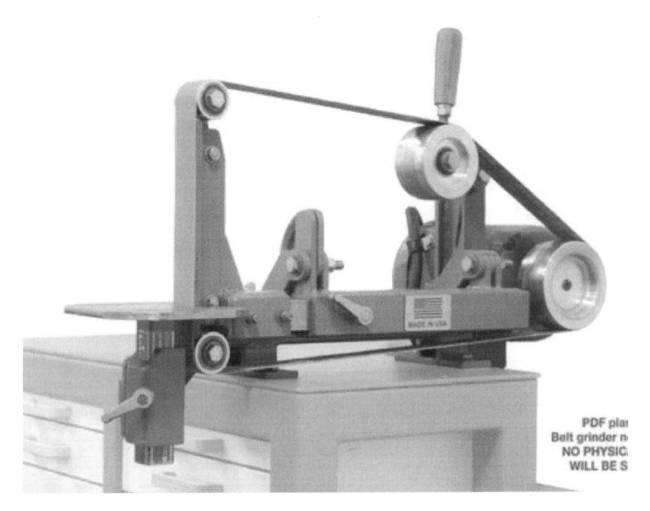

2"X72" Belt Sander

## Quenchant

Quenching is a vital part of the knifemaking process. For the process, you need a container called the 'quenchant.'

During the process of quenching, there is a possibility that your blade could "flare-up," or the oil could begin flaming. For such scenarios, it is always ideal to keep the container used for quenching fireproof. Additionally, you should also make sure that your quench comes with a lid so that you can quickly cut off the supply of oxygen in case of an emergency.

Many people use an improvised container as a quench. You can do the same by using a used metal coffee container. If you are using such a container, then the idea is that you are going to work with blades that can easily fit into the container.

If heat treating 1084 steel, you can use a container of canola oil for quenching.

Other items that you can use as a quench include a 5-gallon steel bucket, a loaf pan, a heavy metal roasting pan, and even a used fire extinguisher with the top part cut off (yeah, that's a thing). But no matter what container you choose, make sure that it is fireproof and has a lid. And oh yes, do not start cutting fire extinguishers without proper equipment and knowledge. It is complex, and you might injure yourself.

## Hacksaw

The hacksaw works similarly to an angle grinder, but it allows you to make fine adjustments whenever you are cutting. You can stop and adjust your position much easier with the hacksaw than with the angle grinder. It also takes longer, since you are doing the cutting by hand.

## Tools for Smithing

There are tools that you will need in your workplace, and there are those tools that you need to have with you in person. They all serve an important purpose, as you will notice when we are working with knives.

Here is something to remember: the number of tools that you can find in a bladesmith's workshop and various purposes that they serve can be quite overwhelming to understand. You might visit a workshop and be amazed at some of the objects you find, wondering just what they can be used for. Since you are a beginner, you don't have to worry about too many tools. You need only to have the below for now.

## Hammer

A bladesmith striking iron with a hammer is, in fact, the quintessential symbolic representation of making a powerful weapon or tool.

There is a reason for that. Your hammer is going to be of the most versatile tool that you are going to use in your knife making process. Think of the hammer as an extension of your arm, reaching out to touch the metal and work with it where your hands cannot (after all, the metals are heated to high temperatures).

Hammering is all about efficiency, so take the time to make your hammer as comfortable as possible. If you have to, you can shave the handle down to fit your hand snugly. You should be able to grasp it easily without having to use a death grip. Your body will get used to working with a particular length, and it helps you become more accurate in time.

One of the most important factors you should consider when choosing a hammer is its weight. It should be light enough that you are not going to cause muscle fatigue. The head of your hammer should weigh anywhere between 1.5 to 3 pounds.

The next thing you should focus on is the length of the handle. It should ideally be the same length as the distance from your elbow to the tips of your fingers. This allows you to work with the metal without keeping close to it.

## Tongs

What the movies don't show you is that many bladesmiths use their tongs. If one hand holds the hammer, the other holds the tongs, even though tongs don't usually get the coverage that they deserve.

In a knife making process, you are usually handling metals that are heated up to 1,500°F. You can't touch metals at that temperature using your gloves. You need special equipment that can hold the metal securely and comfortably.

To put it plainly, you need tongs.

## Anvil

If you are planning to buy a brand-new anvil, then you might have to shell out a little cash. But usually, you will be able to find anvils for sale or being sold second hand. You can get any type of anvil, but beware of any deep chips or indentations that will cause problems when you use it in the future.

Many bladesmiths like using anvils that are at least 100 pounds, but you can use something smaller when first starting out. The one thing I would like to point out is that the lighter the anvil, the more energy it absorbs when you are working with metal. The heavier it is, the more the metal will feel the impact. This is important because you want the metal to feel the impacts rather than the anvil.

## Anvil Stand

This is not vital, but it helps you keep your anvil and the metal steady when you are working. Sometimes, you might experience situations where your anvil can slide along the floor.

The most important reason for getting a stand is to elevate the anvil. Unlike how you see them in movies, the anvil is not that tall. This means you can end up leaning or bending down to work on your metal. Even if you use a chair, you might be in an awkward position to perform your metalworking process. By using a stand, you can raise the anvil for greater comfort.

Want to know the ideal height for your anvil? Place your arms by your side and make a fist. You should place your anvil at the same level as your knuckles.

Another thing that you should focus on is the positioning of your anvil. Ideally, it should be close to your forge but not too close. You should be able to transfer the metal from the forge as quickly as possible with enough room to navigate.

Figure 2: A 55-pound anvil placed on a metal bench.

## Forge

You can typically find two kinds of forges, coal-based, and propane-based. Both have their own set of advantages and limitations.

Coal-Based

These forges are quieter than their propane counterparts. You can also easily get the heat centered around a particular area. This allows them to be truly versatile.

Their drawback is that they are not ideal for beginners. They require a lot of maintenance. If you are not careful or used to them, then they can easily overheat and end up ruining your work. Also, because coal is not particularly clean to handle, you might find them getting dirty quite often.

Propane-Based

The best part about propane-based forge is that they can easily be started and require less time to get used to or work with. They are quite convenient to use and have a higher degree of portability than coal-based forges.

On the flip side, they are quite noisy and require proper ventilation. You should make sure that you are not using propane-based forge inside an enclosed space or there are risks of carbon monoxide poisoning.

The Ideal Forge

If you are getting started, then you could try using a two-brick propane forge. But as mentioned above, make sure that your workspace has proper space. If you are working inside a garage, then make sure that the garage door is wide open to carry out the exhaust and smoke from the propane forge. Additionally, if you are feeling faint or uncomfortable working with a propane forge, then make sure you stop your work, find enough ventilation, move the forge to a different location, and try again.

## Starting With Steel

You are going to come across various steels to work with. There are steels such as 5160, W1, W2, O1, and more. Each type of steel that you find has its own properties.

But which one should you start with? Is there a beginner steel that you can use to practice knife making? Is there a steel that does not pose too many challenges?

Fortunately, there is.

In the world of knifemaking, 1084 is considered a beginner's steel. This steel is one of the most uncomplicated steels that you can work with at home. 1084 is part of the ten series of steels. The higher the number, the higher the percentage of carbon that they have. For example, 1045 has 0.45% carbon out of the total composition of elements in the steel. Here are the remaining steel variations of the ten series:

| 10 Series Steel | Percentage of Carbon |
| --- | --- |
| 1045 | 0.45% |
| 1050 | 0.50% |
| 1055 | 0.55% |
| 1060 | 0.60% |
| 1084 | 0.84% |
| 1095 | 0.95% |

As you can see from the table above, 1084 has enough carbon to give you the sturdiness that you require for your knifemaking. At the same time, it is easier to heat treat 1084. This makes it ideal for getting used to various processes.

Additionally, it takes time to work on other forms of steel. If you start off using a more challenging type of steel and you do not like the results that come out in the end, then you are going to be that much more disappointed and completely exhausted by the entire knife making process. This is why, when you start with the 1084 steel, you won't mind making mistakes.

When you master 1084, you can feel free to move on to 1095, which has a higher carbon content and requires careful attention and skill while going through heat treatment.

# Chapter 2: Anatomy of a Knife

Before you start working on a knife, you need to know more about its anatomy. This knowledge will help you understand just what you are working with and the parts you are going to handle.

## Basic Anatomy

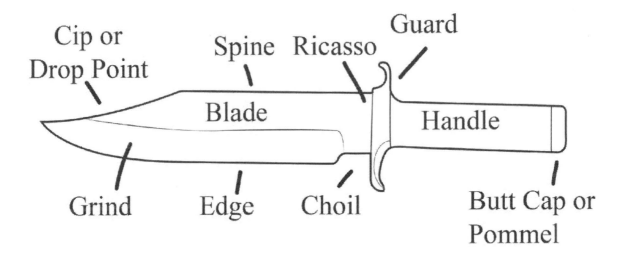

Figure 3: The anatomy of a knife

## Point

The point is the tip of the knife. Or in other words, it is the business end of the knife.

## Belly

The belly of the knife is the arc that is formed along the edge of the knife. It is a curved region that starts from the middle of the knife's blade and reaches the point.

## Spine

This is the unsharpened top part of the knife. Essentially, it is the blunt side that allows people to use their fingers to press down on the knife.

## Edge

The entire sharp part of the blade. Some knives have a single edge while others have a double edge.

## Serrations

Some blades have a sawtooth-like design on the edge of the knife. These designs are often called serrations.

## Blade

The blade is the sharp region of the knife that includes the edge, point, serrations, spine, and belly.

## Bevel

When you look at a knife, then you will notice a slight incline that leads to the edge of the knife. This incline is called the bevel. The higher your bevels are, the more cutting power your knife has.

## Tang

The back portion of the knife. Essentially, this is the 'handle' part of the knife without the actual handle attached to it.

## Handle

The handle is the covering for the tang. The handle can be made out of wood or leather.

## Pin

Not all knives have pins, but they can be spotted easily on the handle of the blade. They are the small spots on the blade which you add to secure the handle to the tang.

## Advanced Anatomy

## Ricasso

This is the thick part of the knife that lies between the blade and the handle. The ricasso is mainly used to provide extra reinforcement of the knife.

## Pommel

This is the butt of the knife, and sometimes, you might find knifemakers turn it into a unique design or a cap-like formation.

## Quillons

These are protrusions from the handle. You will find a pair of these, one on the pommel and one between the ricasso and the handle. They are usually created to prevent the hand from sliding up and down the handle. Can also be referred to as the guard if you see them only formed between the ricasso and the handle.

Quillons are usually designed on only one side of the knife. A guard is formed on both sides of the handle such that if you hold the knife vertically, it will look like a cross. In fact, a better way to imagine this part is to imagine a vertical knife. The horizontal section that goes across the knife is the guard.

## Bolster

With some knives, you might notice a thick junction between the handle of the knife and the blade. This thick section is used to provide a smooth transition from the tang to the blade and is called bolster.

## Choil

Some knives have a slight depression between the edge and the ricasso. Such a depression is known as a choil.

## Knowing the Knife

When you know the different parts of the knife, then it becomes easy for you to design your knife. Do you need a pommel? Are you planning to make a double-edged knife or a single-edge? Since you are a beginner, can you make the guard easily or would you like to try making a knife without a guard first?

By recognizing different parts of the knife, you will be able to create one that fits your idea. Additionally, when you want to make changes to a specific section of a knife, then you will know the name of the part you are focusing on. This becomes important when you are trying to describe your knife to someone else.

## Blade Profiles

Different knives will be better suited for various tasks, depending on their blade profile. The profile is the term used to describe the overall shape of the blade and gives the blade its look. Learning the basic blade profiles can serve as a guide while designing your blade based on the specific functions you want it to serve.

One of the most common blade profiles is the drop point, which is favored as the best style for survival and hunting blades. A drop point is characterized by the spine of the blade "dropping" down from the handle to the tip, with the tip at the center axis of the blade. The spine extends the full length of the tip, which makes it much stronger and less prone to breaking. It also makes an excellent knife for carving.

A clip point blade is another common type of blade profile and is named after the "clipped off" appearance of the tip of the blade. The tip is sharper and thinner and, therefore, more suited for stabbing and piercing. However, this thin tip also makes it much weaker than a drop point blade, and it tends to break more easily.

A tanto profile is sometimes used in a military-style design and fighting utility knives. This profile has a spine that slopes slightly down to a point that is sharp and angular. This makes for a blade with a tip that is great for piercing, stabbing, and general utility.

A spearpoint design has a point that meets in the middle of two symmetrical sides, much like the tip of a spear. A spearpoint can have either one or both edges sharpened and has a strong and sharp point. This feature makes it a great knife for piercing or stabbing. However, it's very difficult to do any fine carving or detail work with, and it isn't a practical daily-use knife.

## Designing a Knife

There are a few things that you should remember when you are designing your knife.

When you are designing a knife, make sure you know what you will primarily use it for. This helps you understand how you would like to design the edge, whether you need a guard, what kind of point you should create, and other useful information. A lot of people who start making knives think that they would like to design a knife that can achieve practically every purpose. But such a knife does not exist. Designing a knife in a particular manner means that you have to make sacrifices in other areas.

To make a knife, you will require a knife template. The best way to learn how to make a template is to see it in the process. So, here are the steps to create your very own knife template. In this template, we are going to create a simple hunting knife.

On a piece of printer paper, draw two horizontal lines that are no more than 2 inches apart. Since you are getting started, use a width of 1¼ inch. Between these two lines, you have to create your knife.

The overall length of the knife should not be more than 15 inches. However, with our measurements, the knives won't even be that long.

Let's focus on the blade first. A 4-inch blade might be too long for some and anything that falls below 3¼ inches might be too short. Mainly, you should keep the blade length at 3⅞ inches or if that seems too precise, then make the blade between 3¼ and 4 inches long.

Creating the handle is tricky since different people have different hand sizes. But what you should do is form a handle that balances the blade. At this point, you should ideally be looking to create a handle that is about 4 inches long. Some knife makers can go up to 4¼ inches long for the handle, but you should remain within the 4 ¼ inch mark.

## Creating a Template

First of all, gather the things you need to make your design.

You only need a ruler, paper and a pencil.

When you are designing a knife, make sure you know what you will primarily use it for.

This helps you understand how you would like to design the edge, whether you need a guard, what kind of point you should create, and other useful information.

A lot of people who start making knives think that they would like to design a knife that can achieve practically every purpose.

This will never be the case.

Designing a knife in a particular manner means that you have to make sacrifices in other areas.

For this project we are making a drop point hunting knife.

The drop point hunting knife is the favorite of many knifemakers and a staple project for beginners.

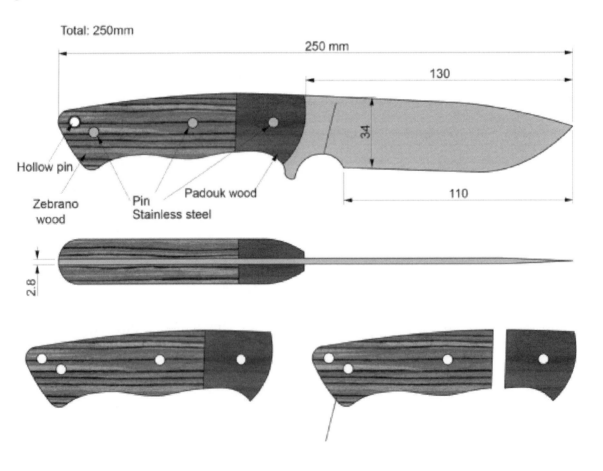

If you want to get the printable version of this knife template for FREE, go to **https://www.forge-hero.com/free-bonus**, and enter your e-mail.

We have chosen the drop point design for the following reasons:

**Pros of a drop point blade:**

- Long, uninterrupted cutting edge
- The tip is sharp enough to perform precision work.
- The tip is lowered, so you have excellent control over it.
- The drop point style sports a large belly, so slicing is a piece of cake.
- Because the back is relatively straight, this knife is great for batoning.
- This is an all-around knife that can perform most tasks.
- This is an excellent option for your hunting knife.
- This is also an excellent knife for everyday carrying.
- If you have this knife during a survival or tactical situation, you are going to be set.

**Cons of a drop point blade:**

- The point is pretty broad, so stabbing isn't going to be a piece of cake.

**THE STEPS**

**Step 1:** First, design the profile for the piece of steel you will. For this project, we are using a 0.3X4X25 cm piece of 1085 steel (roughly 0.12X1.5X10 inch).

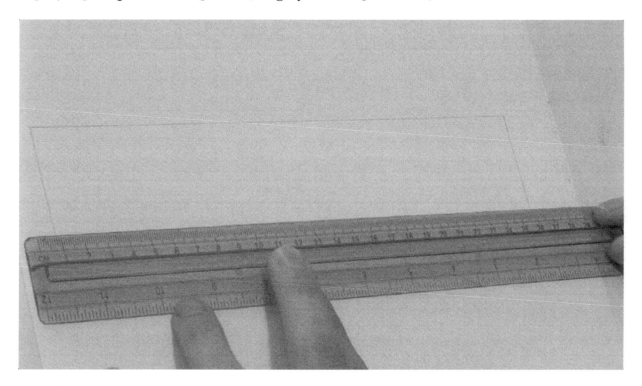

**Step 2:** Decide the size of the handle by measuring the size of hand. This will make sure the handle will fit your hand.

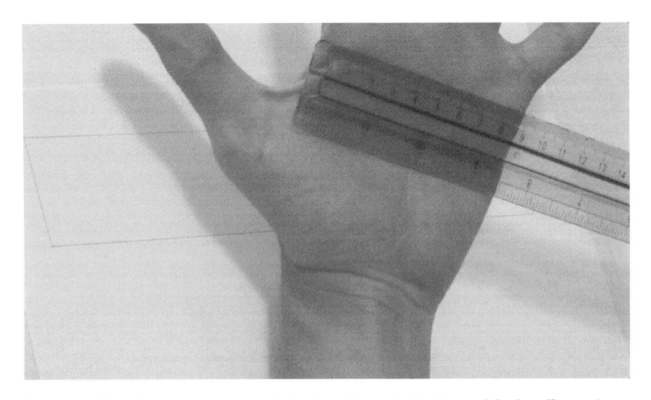

**Step 3:** Add to the measure 1cm in the back and 3cm in the front of the handle portion.

First add in the 1cm gap.

Then the length of the handle.

Finally 3cm gap in front of handle. Divide the diagram into two parts from that point, like shown above.

**Step 4:** From the rest of the steel length decide your blade length. Keep some space between the blade and the handle to form the choil.

First, mark the choil.

The rest of the length left in the diagram will be your blade length.

In this project we have handle length as 9cm and blade length 11cm.

**Step 5:** Decide where you want your tip. This will be your drop point.

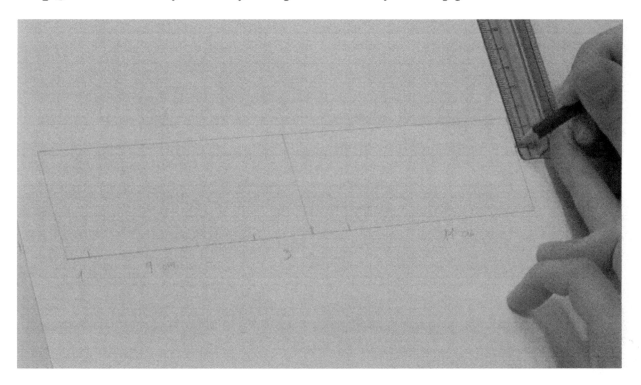

First mark the drop point.

Then join it to form the blade profile, like shown in the picture above.

Then draw out the choil.

**Step 6:** Now for the handle, draw a line slightly higher than the bottom of the steel billet.

**Step 7:** Draw the handle design using that bottom line as a guide.

Don't worry about the accuracy of your drawing. After you finish drawing, you can modify the lines until you like the final result.

**Step8:** Draw the end of the handle using the line drawn previously as reference.

**Step 9:** In case you're making a composite handle or adding a bolster to your design, decide where the division of the materials will be.

For this project we will have a composite wood handle made of zebran and padouk wood.

**Step 10:** Decide where the pins will be. Make sure that they are spaced evenly.

**If you're using a bolster make sure that the bolster area has one pin hole**.

This will ensure that the bolster is secured well with the tang.

We are also adding a 6mm hole for a hollow pin in our design. This is an optional addition to your design.

**And that's pretty much it!**

Congratulations! you have designed your very own knife template.

If you want more ready-made designs you can simply print and use the check out our **5-Second Knife Templates,** at <u>forge-hero.com/5secknifetemplates</u>

Have questions? Send in your doubts to **support@forge-hero.com** and we will be sure to respond!

Using a band saw, or hacksaw, carefully cut out the design onto the piece of wood. Fine-tune the template by using a wood file to get rid of the saw marks and shape your knife by taking away everything up to the edge of the drawing. The more precise you are, the more you'll get a feel for what your knife will be like.

Hold the template in your hand and get a feel for it. Does the handle need to be longer or shorter? Is the blade length what you're looking for? Are the blade length and handle length the right proportions? If you have any doubts in the design, this is the time to fix it. It takes far less time to make a new template than to try to fix design flaws in your blade as you're working.

# Chapter 3: Making a Knife By Stock Removal

In this chapter, we are going to learn how to make a knife using a method that is ideal for beginners; stock removal.

We have already created the template for the hunting knife in the previous chapter. The topic of grinding bevels and heat treatment are explained in more detail, later in this book.

As we had mentioned before, we are going to start off by using the 1085 billet. We already know the dimensions of our knife, so it should be relatively easy to discover the dimensions of the steel as well.

**Step 1:** First, cut out the shape of the knife.

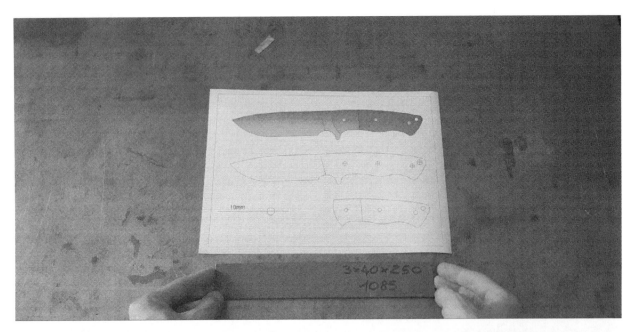

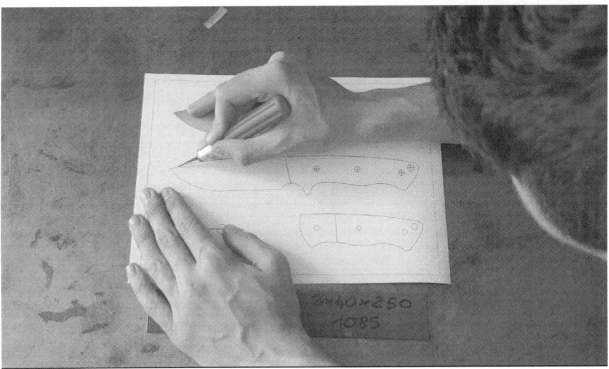

**Step 2:** Take some tracing liquid (in this case we use dykem blue), a scribe pen and some magnets. Paint the entire surface of the steel billet with dykem using a brush.

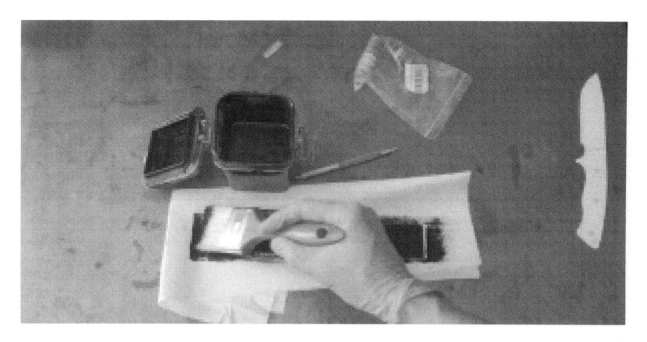

**Step 3:** Lay the template in place and secure it with magnets. You can also paste it if you don't have magnets, but magnets keep it clean and are cheap.

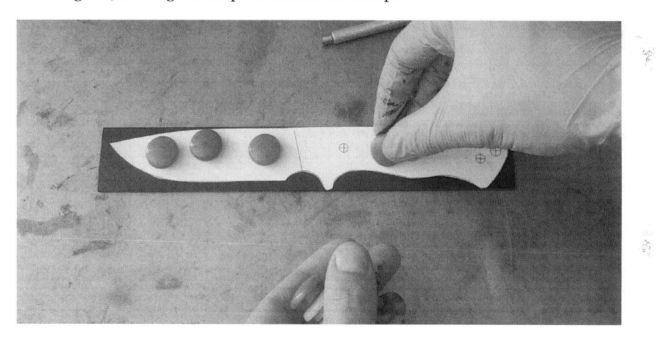

**Step 4:** Trace the outline of the template with the scribe pen.

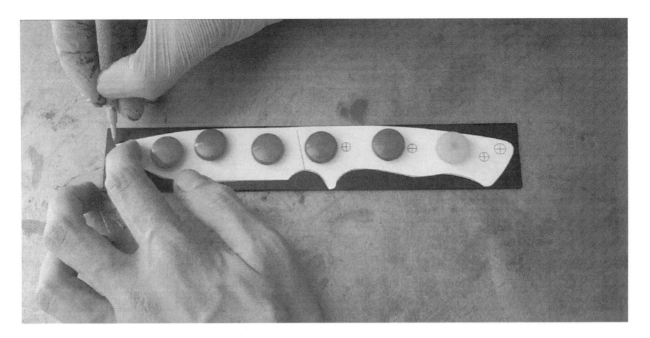

**Step 5:** Now using a hole punch and a hammer, lightly punch in the hole marks in the template.

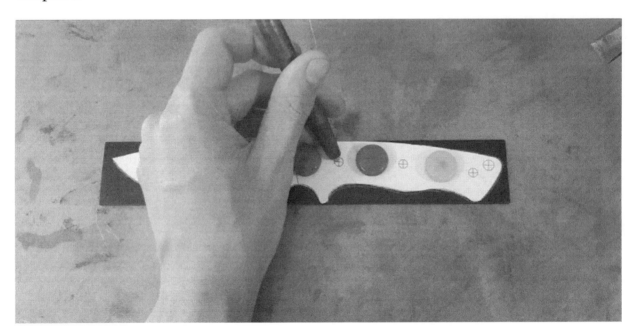

**Step 6:** Now we are ready to cut the template out. In this video, we use a bandsaw and a 2"X72" belt grinder to do so, but if you're on a low budget then you can just as easily use a hacksaw and an angle grinder.

First, roughly cut out the template using the bandsaw.

Next, we make the fine adjustments using the belt grinder.

For stock removal we will use a 100 grit ceramic belt.

Be careful not to press too hard against the grinder. Focus on lightly passing the steel across the surface of the grinder.

just aim to take some material off with each pass off the grinder.

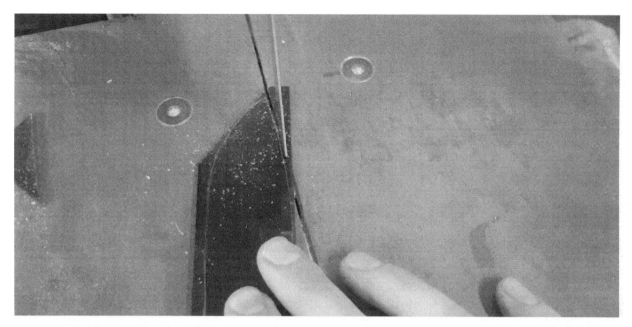

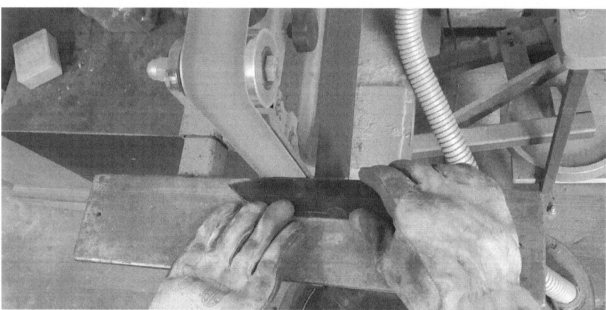

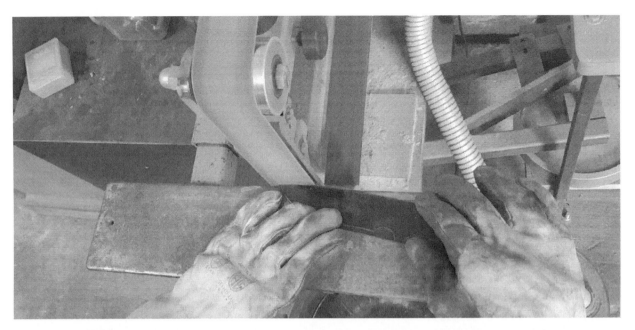

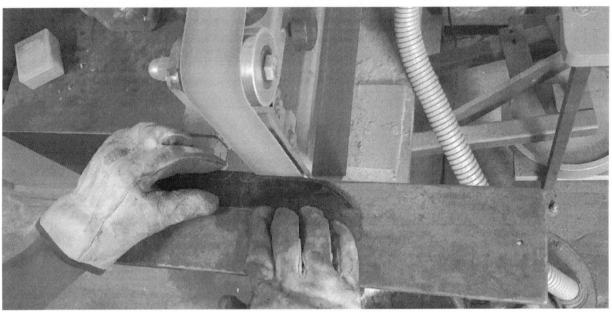

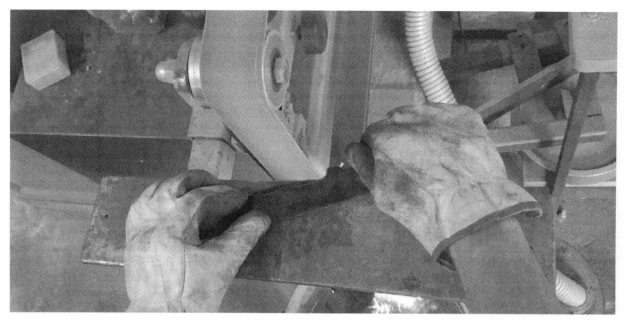

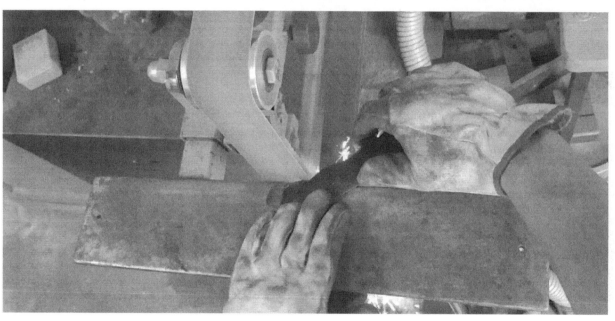

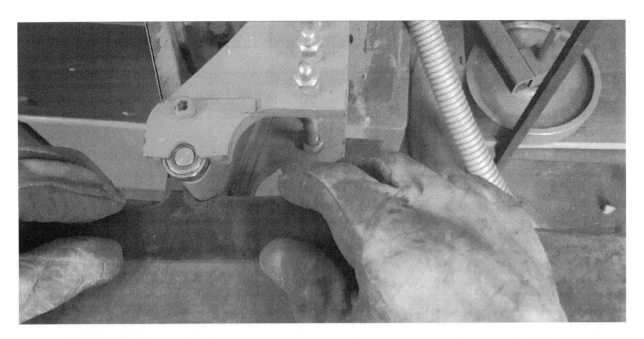

For grinding the smaller and rounder curves of the template, you can use a file, in case you don't have a belt grinder and a small roll attachment.

**Step 7:** We move to drilling the holes on the tang. Use can use a hand drill instead of the drill press we show in the video.

While drilling the steel make sure that you use a drill bit that 0.5mm larger than the size mentioned in the template.

This will make sure that the hole is slightly larger than the handle holes and facilitate gluing of the handle.

**Step 8:** Finish off the holes with a countersink, or alternatively with a drill that is double the size of the previous drill bit. Make sure you don't drill too deep.

**Step 9:** Congratulations! You're knife blank is ready for grinding.

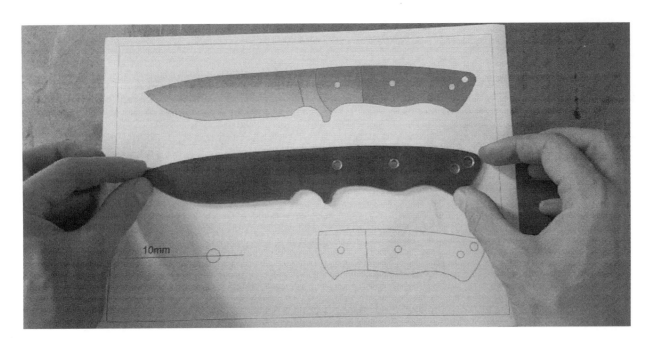

## A Couple of Tips to Remember

- You can also drill holes into the knife design that you made on the steel bar before using a hacksaw to cut it. This is because it is much easier to clamp down a rectangular piece of steel, as compared to a knife blank.
- When you are working on the belt sander, make sure that your tool rest is as close to the belt as possible. If it is not, then there is a possibility that the belt with catch the knife, wrestle it in between, and harm your fingers in the process.

# Chapter 4: Forging a Knife (Full Tang Knife)

Before we go into the actual process of forging, it is better to understand a bit about the process.

After all, you have your workspace all set up, your design laid out, and a piece of steel ready to go. At this point, you should make sure all your tools are where you can have easy access to them, place your blade in the forge, and get it cranking.

To properly work your blade, you'll need to take it out of the forge when it's at an appropriate temperature. While it's possible to buy a thermometer for a propane forge, most people gauge the right temperature and the degree of workability of the metal by its color.

Here is a table to help you understand the color and the temperature of the metal when it attains that color. Use this as a reference whenever you work with your metal.

| Fahrenheit | The Color of the Steel | Process |
|---|---|---|
| 2,000° | Bright Yellow | Forging |
| 1,900° | Dark Yellow | Forging |
| 1,800° | Orange Yellow | Forging |
| 1,700° | Orange | Forging |
| 1,600° | Orange Red | Forging |
| 1,500° | Bright Red | Forging |
| 1,400° | Red | Forging |
| 1,300° | Medium Red | - |
| 1,200° | Dull Red | - |
| 1,100° | Slight Red | - |
| 1,000° | Mostly Grey | - |
| 800° | Dark Grey | Tempering |
| 575° | Blue | Tempering |
| 540° | Dark Purple | Tempering |
| 520° | Purple | Tempering |

| 480° | Brown | Tempering |
|------|-------|-----------|
| 445° | Light Straw | Tempering |

Remember that when you are using the table, you don't have to get the exact shade of the color mentioned above. Typically, if you get an orange-yellow or orange shade, then you have reached the orange temperature range. Which is why you might always hear bladesmiths mention that they heat the metal to a particular range.

We are going to use the same knife design that we created in Chapter 2. If you haven't designed the knife already, go ahead and create the design now.

Once again, we are going to use a steel that is 9 inches long and 2 inches wide. This time, however, we are going to use 1095 high carbon steel.

We are going to begin by de-scaling the steel. The method to de-scale is taught in Chapter 3. After you have completed de-scaling the steel, here are the steps that you need to take to forge it.

Here are a couple of things to remember:

- Steel needs to undergo changes during heating to become malleable (or flexible in layman terms, but we do not use the term flexible here as it might indicate the metal can be stretched). If you try to hit a piece of steel that's too cold, you'll only be working the outer layers of the metal, and you'll get a unique effect that looks like mushroom shapes taking place on the metal.
- It's also possible to get too high of a temperature, which is most likely when using a coal forge. As a beginner, you should start with the propane forge but if you are already using the coal forge, then make sure that you are careful and not overheating the metal. Here is a tip for you to follow when you are using a coal-based forge: take care to arrange your coals so that you can lay your steel across the fire evenly. If you concentrate the heat towards the knife to a particular area, then it is possible to melt the tip of your knife entirely off. Or an easier method is to, of course, use a propane forge!

## A Game Plan

Before you start hammering, you need to come up with a game plan. Your steel will begin to cool down immediately when you take it out of the forge, and every time you place it on the anvil, it rapidly draws heat away through conduction. This means you only have about six to eight good hammer strikes before you need to put it back in again to heat up. So if you are in the process of shaping the metal, then you have to be precise with your strikes. Use your time wisely! Take a good look at your steel and plan exactly where you'll be hitting it before you put it back in the forge. Make a mental plan of the steps you'll be taking so that you don't have to waste any time trying to figure that out when your blade is heated and ready to work. If you do have to stop hammering for a moment, hold the steel up instead of letting it rest on the anvil to prevent unnecessary cooling.

As a beginner, your ability to make accurate strikes on the metal is unlikely. You might not be able to get the shape that you want quickly. But that is okay. Take as much time as you need and place the metal into the forge through multiple cycles to form the shape you had in your mind.

There are no mistakes here, merely lessons to be learned while you work the forge.

## Working With Steel

It's useful to think of the hot steel as clay. Imagine hitting clay with your hammer and what would happen to it as you delivered blows. While steel will be a lot harder to move than clay, the basic principles are the same. As you apply force, the malleable steel will move away from that force in the direction of least resistance. As you work, you will be adjusting where you are striking with your hammer as well as the direction of your strike. In this manner, you can control not only the force but where the steel will have a tendency to move by manipulating the path of least resistance.

As you work, the steel will eventually bend up at the ends, losing its flatness. It seems like common sense to want to hammer on the upturned ends to flatten the steel again, but this doesn't allow you to apply the right kind of force. By flipping the steel over and striking it in the middle, both ends will be pushed flat against the anvil as the middle moves away from the force of your hammer. Keep an eye on the steel as you work. Use the last strike or two to ensure your steel stays as flat as possible.

Now we are going to see how you can use the forge to give shape to the knife.

1. The first thing you are going to do is figure out where the knife's tip is going to be. Since we are not going to be using the hacksaw and grinding the knife, we are going to be using the forge to shape out the knife.
2. Heat the steel until it reaches the yellow temperature range.
3. Once it reaches the temperature, use your tongs to take out the steel. Now you are going to hold the steel on the anvil. Hold it in a way that the future cutting edge of the knife is facing down.
4. Hit the top corner at a 45° angle. This is because we are going to start with the knife's drop point, which is an easy way to create the knife point. As you strike, you'll notice the steel mushrooming out. When you see this happen, then place the steel on its sides and hammer it until the mushroom shape disappears.

Figure 6: Forging the right knife is all about patience and careful understanding of the technique.

5. Go back to the previous position and continue hammering the steel at a 45° angle.
6. Keep repeating this process until you have what looks like the profile of the knife tip pounded in.
7. Currently, the point or tip of the knife will be positioned more towards where the edge of the knife should be. This tip will change position as you continue to move the metal, moving from the bottom of the blade to the top. The natural tendency of the metal is to push things away as it gets thinner, which is why, as you begin working on the edge, this tip or point will end up rising to the top of the blade, closer to the blade's spine level.

So if you start getting worried about why your point is not in the correct position, don't! We still have a lot of steps to go.

8. So back to the knife. We are now going to work on the knife's edge.
9. Look at your steel again and decide how long you want the cutting edge of your knife to be. This is based on the total length of the knife's blade. So you should have placed it anywhere between 3¼ inches and 4 inches long.
10. Once you have decided the length of the knife, heat it again until it reaches the yellow temperature range.
11. Here is a trick that you can use to make a mark on the blade so that you will know where the blade of the knife begins. Hold the blade over the edge of the anvil and hit one side of it (the spindle side of the knife) of it with the hammer to make a small indented mark on

the cutting edge side of the blade. This mark will let you know where the handle of the blade starts from (make sure that you are using your measurements to decide where this mark should be). You can choose to remove this mark later during the forging process (it happens as you work on the metal) or alternatively, many bladesmiths make the indentation deeper and make a choil out of it. For now, we are going to focus on how to make a basic knife without the choil.

12. Now that you know the edge. It is time to hammer it out and make it look sharp!

13. **Tip:** Use a little bit of water on the anvil. This will help blow out the knife scale, with each hammer blow.

14. Holding your steel flat on the anvil, pound along the edge. Flip the metal and hammer on the same part from the other side. This will cause the metal here to thin out and will begin to create the bevels of your knife. Notice how, as you thin the edge, the tip will slowly start moving up towards the spine side of the knife. This means that you are going to get the point to the proper place.

15. As you make progress with your blade, keep an eye on its overall shape. In addition to maintaining overall flatness, you'll have to work to keep the spine of your blade straight as well. As you notice it losing its straightness, flip the blade onto its edge so that the spine is on the anvil. Now hammer the spine until you see it becoming straight. But won't this affect the edge as well? Of course, it will! In which case, flip the knife onto its side and hammer the edge back to its correct shape. You need to constantly correct the shapes of either parts of the blade.

16. As you keep working on the metal, you will notice that it will get a rough shape. You don't have to work until the edge is truly sharp. All you are doing is getting a rough outline of the final knife that you are going to work on.

17. Once you get a rough shape, shift your attention to the handle area, or tang. Hold the blade on its edge, with the spine side on the anvil.

18. Start hammering the knife from the part where your indentation starts (the one you used to mark the start of the blade). Once again, hammer the side of the blade to remove the mushrooming effect that the metal gains during the process. Before working on the tang, the edge and the tang will look like they are connected. Once you start hammering the knife, the tang will form a handle shape, the metal getting narrower.

19. By now, you should be able to see the full shape of your knife starting to form. Use the techniques you've learned to try to focus on areas that show mistakes and further refine the profile of your knife. There's no substitution for time and learning from your mistakes, so don't be afraid if you make them. Every mistake is an opportunity to learn.

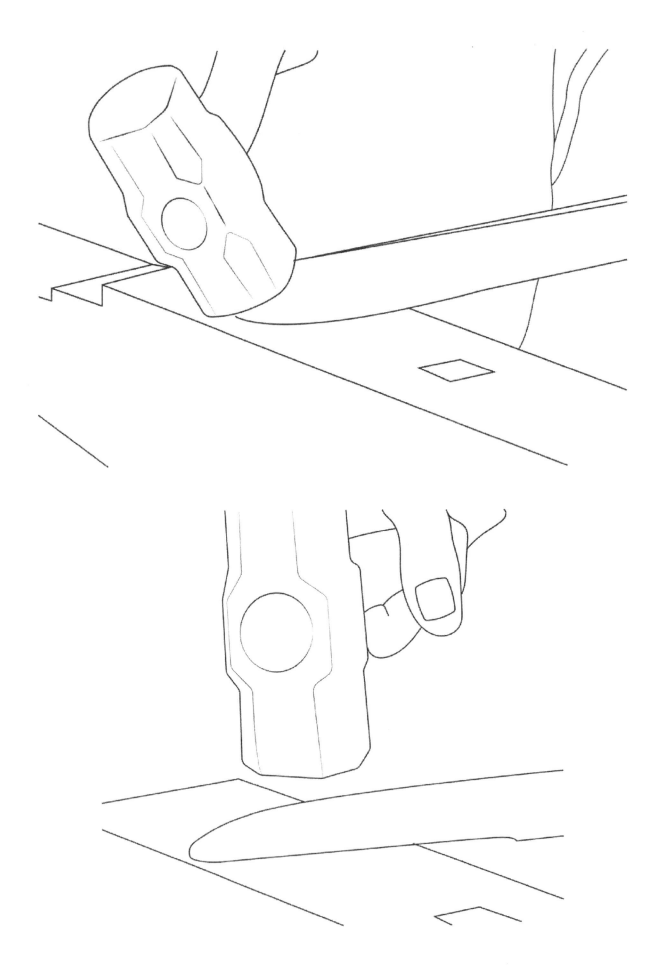

Figure 7 & 8: Hit the steel at the corners to develop the point

20. Once you have completed the profile of your knife and you are satisfied with the results, let's move on to making holes in the tang.

21. You have already seen how you can make holes using the drill. But since your knife is hot, how can you create these holes right now? What you do is use a technique called the hot punch. How does it work? Let's find out.

22. The first thing that you are going to want to do is get yourself a hot punch, which is like a pointed and elongated piece of steel. Look at the pointed end of the hot punch and check out how narrow or broad it is. This will let you know how big the hole on the tang will be.

23. When you are ready, heat the knife's tang until it reaches the yellow range in temperature. Once the temperature is right, place the knife on the anvil. Focus on where you would like to create a hole in the tang. Place the hot punch on top of that position and strike it a few times. Flip the knife over with the tongs, and you will be able to notice a small dark spot where the punch struck the knife on the other side. Place the punch over this dark spot and hit it with the hammer. Continue this process until you literally 'punch' out the piece of metal from the tang and create a hole. Make sure to take the hot punch out quickly after hammering, so that it does not get stuck in the hole and join with the knife.

24. Repeat this step with the rest of the holes that you would like to create on the knife.

25. At this point, you might notice that your knife might have some scaling on it. Head over to the grinder and remove the scales (you can also use the white vinegar method, but at this point, the scales won't be too challenging to remove).

26. Once we have accomplished all of that, it is time to move on to the next step: grinding bevels!

# Chapter 5: Grinding Good Bevel Lines

Now that making the knife blank is done, it's time to start grinding. After the profile of your knife is refined, you'll be removing layers of knife material to create bevels. These will form an angle that makes the cutting edge of your blade.

You could say that this is the defining moment in which you turn your piece of steel into a knife. Does that sound exciting? Well, let's get started. But before that, we should understand a little more about grinding.

There's a variety of tools and techniques you can use to create these grinds, and your choice will depend on your own experience and preference. Professional knifemakers make this step look easy, but it takes a lot of practice to develop their level of comfort and skill. The trick is to go slow, be patient with yourself, and put in plenty of time behind the grinder.

Before you start making the angles, make sure your blade profile is all set. You can remove any large pieces of steel outside your design with a hacksaw, band saw, or the cutting wheel of an angle grinder. If you worked your blade at the forge, then revisit the template and redraw your bevel line. Use a belt grinder, files, or angle grinder to remove all material that won't be part of your knife's final shape.

A quality grind on a knife is produced not only with great technique but with a basic understanding of blade geometry. A good blade has an appropriate balance between overall strength, sharpness, and edge retention suited for its intended use. Unfortunately, there's no one-size-fits-all knife grind. Understanding what factors affect the performance of your blade will help you to choose the best grind for your blade and allow you to have a specific goal in mind.

The first thing that you will notice is that there are different types of grinds that you can use for your blade. Here are the most popular ones:

## Full Flat Grind

This grind is done in a V-shaped and works consistently from the spine to the edge. It creates a good balance of cutting ability and strength. While it is a very sharp grind, it can dull quickly but is easy to sharpen. This design is standard in kitchen knives.

## Scandinavian Grind

Often used when making bushcraft knives, the Scandinavian grind - or Scandi grind for short - is a flat grind that starts below the halfway point of the blade. By leaving a lot of material in the spine of the blade, this grind can maximize the durability of your knife. The lack of a secondary bevel means that the low angle will create a sharp edge. While the edge is not as tough as other grinds that offer a secondary bevel, it does make it very easy to sharpen in the field, even for a beginner. It is an excellent grind for carving.

The location of the bevel makes it easy to see what you're doing, and a blade with a Scandi grind will be able to cut through most pieces of wood with relative ease.

Scandi

## Sabre Grind

The sabre grind is a flat grind that starts halfway up the blade. While it isn't quite as good at carving, it tends to slice slightly better. Unlike the Scandi, the sabre grind typically has a secondary bevel.

Sabre
Grind

## Hollow Grind

In this grind, the bevels curve in to form a thin, very sharp edge. This edge tends not to be as durable as some other grinds, and it tends to need a lot of retouching to stay sharp. This edge can be slightly more challenging to grind as a knifemaker, but the edge created isn't difficult to re-sharpen.

The incredible sharp edge of a hollow grind makes it the grind of choice for straight razors and hunting knives. It tends to bind up at the top of the hollow when slicing through materials such as cardboard and isn't as well suited to being a utility knife as some other grind styles.

Full
Hollow
Grind

## Convex Grind

A convex grind is a rounded grind that focuses on the edge. The mass behind the edge increases the durability of the edge, and it can be quite sharp. This grind is often used in axes, machetes, or choppers.

Convex
Grind

## Chisel Grind

In a chisel grind, one side of the cutting edge has a flat grind, while the other has no bevel ground in. Because of the shallow blade angle, a chisel grind makes an incredibly sharp edge. This sharp angle also means the edge doesn't have the best durability and needs to be continuously maintained. Chisel grinds are commonly used in food preparation as well as woodworking, as the bevel makes it easy to follow the wood grain. It can be slightly inaccurate when slicing, due to the edge being off-center. Knives made with this grind are often either right-handed blades or left-handed blades, depending on which side the bevel is on.

Chisel
Grind

Figures 9 to 13: Different grinds and their profiles

## A Note Before Grinding

When you spend more time grinding, you develop an instinctual understanding of how your body needs to move to get the results you want. There is definitely a learning curve, so be patient with yourself. With a little bit more time, you won't need to think about your movements as much as when you're first starting.

Developing your grinding style is about consistency, so eliminate discomforts. Stand with a slightly wide-set but comfortable stance to give yourself a stable base. Keep your elbows tucked against your sides and lock them into your hips. Instead of using your arms to move the blade, move from your core. Shift your weight steadily in your hips and think about using controlled and calculated movements. By working to create a pattern in your movement, you will find a comfortable rhythm that will make grinding much more predictable.

Finally, make sure that you do not take any substantial risks. Be patient with your work and make sure that you are comfortable understanding the basics of grinding.

## Creating a Grind

**Step 1:** Mark the bevel you want you want on your knife with dykem blue. Also mark the edge of your knife with dykem blue.

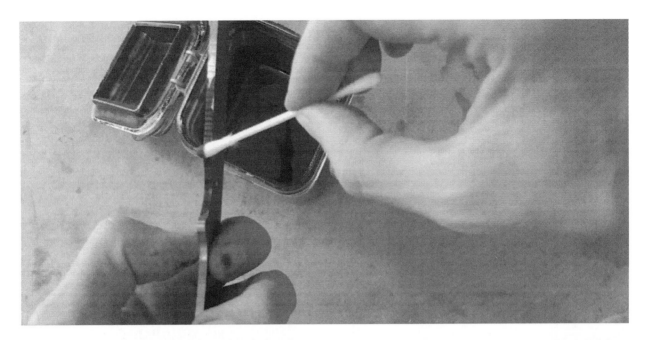

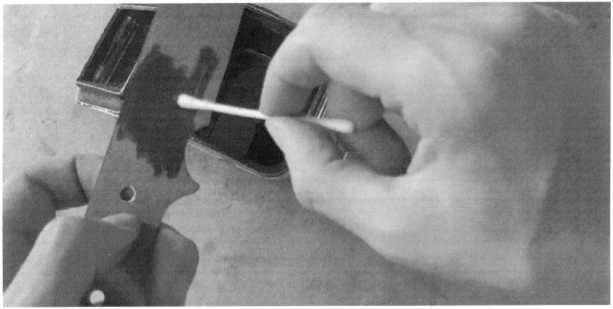

**Step 2:** Cut out the bevel part from the template and place it on the steel.

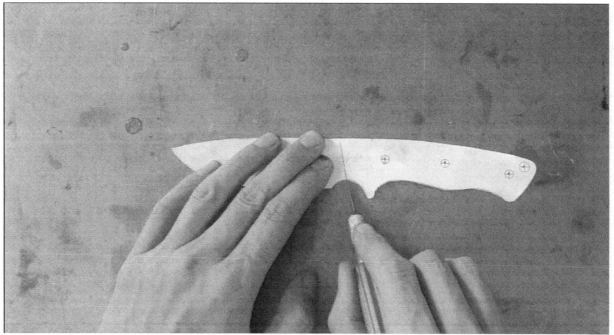

**Step 3:** Scribe the end of the cut out to mark the end of the bevel.

**Step 4:** After scribing, attach a file guide right along that line. This way you will never grind too far away from the bevel and ensures you have clean grind lines.

**Step 5: Now we move on to bevel grinding.**

Before we start let us review the technique. For this project we will be doing a flat grind.

**Pros of flat grind:**

Flat ground blades have the advantage of being very sharp and extremely easy to sharpen on a flat stone and in the field

## Cons:

The disadvantage is that the edge isn't terribly durable and will (turn) dull quickly

## How to do a flat grind:

- The right hand controls the blade while the left thumb presses the area of the knife you want to grind.

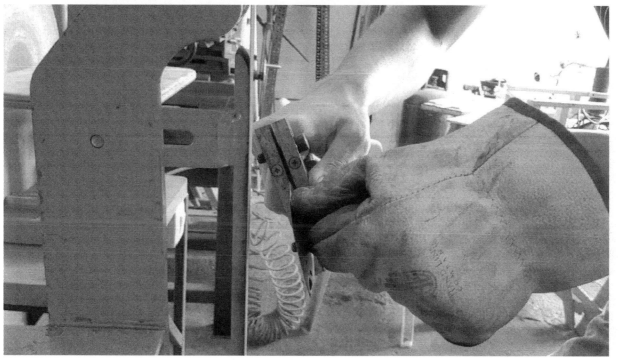

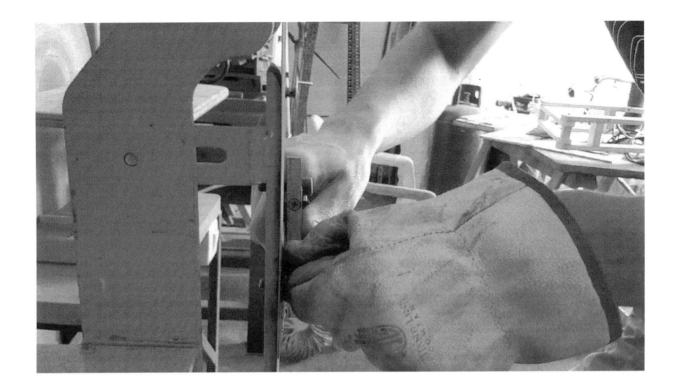

- Press the blade against the belt and move sideways, along the entire length of the bevel.
- Cool the blade in water from time to time, to keep it from overheating. If an area of the blade starting to change color, it's a sign that the steel is getting overheated.
- Aim to take out a small amount of material with each pass of the blade

- Repeat the grind on the other side.

- If you want a thinner spine, like we have in this project, you can simply flip the knife and do the same grind with the spine area of the knife.

- Make sure that you keep your elbows close and your hips tight.

**Once the grinding is finished,**

**Step 6:** Sand the knife blank with 220 grit sandpaper to remove any dykem marks on the steel.

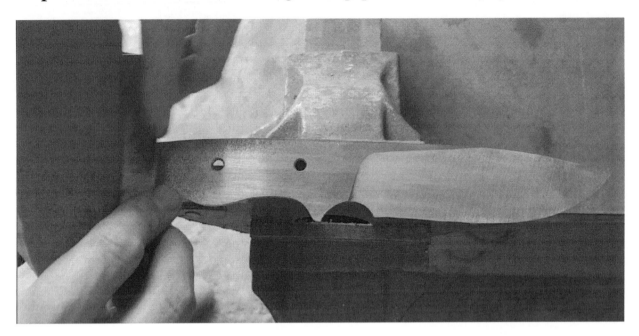

Let us work with the Scandi grind technique and then you can use the same ideas for the other grinds:

- The first thing that you need to do is create the bevel outline in the metal. To do this, take out a permanent marker and then find the center line of your cutting edge.
- Mark that outline. If you like, you can even color the entire edge of the blade using the marker.

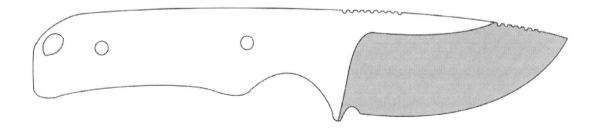

Figure 14: Mark the entire area you want to grind

- The next part is a little tricky, so make sure you read this instruction carefully before putting it to practice. Take a hand drill (or scribe) close to the outline of your blade (near the center) and run it along the flat surface, dragging the tip along the blade edge.

- ○ Let's imagine that you are creating a knife that is 2 inches wide. You have decided to draw the outline at the 1-inch mark.
- ○ You are going to use the drill to create a line just below the outline (this process is called scribing), allowing you to see where you would like the bevels to meet. Flip the blade and do the same thing again.
- ○ Now you can mark the bevel outline on the blade.
- ○ Alternatively, you can use only the outline for the purpose, but by creating a mark, you have a better idea of where you should start the bevel.
- ○ This step makes sure that the grinds will be symmetrical, and more resistant to warping after heat treatment.
- We are now going to take the knife to the grinder. If your grinder does not have a fresh belt, then it might be time to get one. This is because old belts heat up faster. However, you can still work using an old belt as well as it will teach you the effects of overheating, and when you should take the blade away from the belt. As for the belt grit, you can use a 50 grit belt for this purpose.
- Bring the steel toward the belt. Gently let the steel find the spot you've created for the edge and start moving the steel gently sideways. You don't need to place a ton of pressure on the blade; move it across and let the belt do its job.

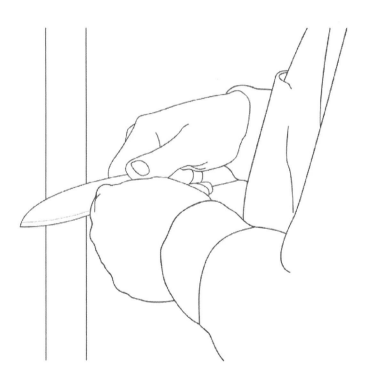

Figure 15: Sideways grinding

- Every time you take your steel off the grinder, assess how much material you need to take off and repeat the process. You should always have a clear idea of this before you grind again. Many knifemakers make the mistake of jumping back to grinding without a second thought, and end up either taking out too much material, or messing up the grind lines.
- Do not focus on one side only. Keep flipping the knife over to keep the grind lines even.
- Allow the grind to pass across the full length of the cutting edge, from the tip to just before the where the outline ends and the tang begins.
- Switch sides every few passes to keep the grind lines even.
  - Some knifemakers start at the end of the outline and work their way toward the tip of the knife. Other makers do the complete opposite; starting from the tip and moving along the knife towards the tang. There is no right or wrong way here.
  - Try working the blade both ways and see which you prefer. Remember, you are allowed to make as many mistakes as possible. Once you find the method that is comfortable for you, it will become easier for you in future grinds. But the only way you are going to find out the comfort point is by actually experimenting with different grinds!
- Another important tip to remember at this point: keep even pressure on the blade, and keep the steel moving. Check your progress every few passes. But do not be tempted to stop and check every few seconds, as this might cause the grinding process to give you a choppy line.
- Continue working your grind higher and higher up toward the spine. Every pass should be slightly higher than the last. Your grind lines should be as straight as possible.
- If you notice your line becoming wavy, try and check the amount of pressure you're putting on the blade and try to keep it consistent.
- If you find a specific area has less material taken off, try slowing down on those high spots and putting more pressure on the other side of the blade.
- Work on the blade slowly so that you can keep things even on both sides of the knife.
- Here is a tip you can use if you don't mind spending a little for different grits for your grinder.
  - Start with a 50 grit belt and complete the grinding process until the previous step.
  - Once done, switch out your 50 grit belt for a 120 grit and color in the ground surface with a permanent marker again. Take your blade back to the grinder and start to clean up your grinds with the finer grit.
  - Keep working until the marker is completely removed and then repeat the process with a 220 grit.
  - This process of cleaning up the grind isn't only about the aesthetic of the blade but is a precautionary measure taken to prevent the blade from cracking or warping in the heat treat.
  - Any deep grooves, scratches, or sharp edges will be susceptible to cracking in the quench due to the stress created by this process. As a bonus, this will likely make the blade easier to clean up after the heat treatment process.

# The Hollow Ground Edge

The hollow ground edge has a concave edge. This form of an edge is well suited to blades that will be mainly used for slicing. Examples of such blades include skinners, hunters, filet knives, etc.

The main reason why the hollow ground edge is suitable for such knives is the fact that it produces a very thin edge that can be sharpened quite easily. However, because of this thin edge, the blade can be somewhat fragile compared to other forms of grinds. This is why it is not prudent to make a hollow ground edge if you are going to be using your blade against heavier substances such as bone, wood, or materials with similar thickness. An important fact to know here is most of the blades produced around the world today are hollow ground. It could be because not many people are looking to cut bone or thicker materials!

Here is how you can achieve a hollow grind. Follow the steps in the process for the Scandi edge until you come to the part where you begin grinding. The process will be a little different for the Scandi grind.

- Take the blade and slowly bring the edge to the surface of the wheel of the belt.
- Now start the wheel of the belt and allow for the grind to form. Flip the knife over and then work on the other side. That is essentially the basics of the hollow grind edge. For beginners, getting the perfect grind might not be easy. However, with practice, you should be able to get the edge that you require.

## The Flat Grind

The flat grind creates a nice balance between the hollow grind and the convex grind. One of the main advantages it provides is that, since it draws from both the hollow grind and the convex grind, it has an excellent edge that can bear the brunt of heavy chopping. Additionally, even after multiple chopping sessions, it can still retain its sharpness.

- The flat grind is similar to the hollow grind but is simpler to perform. This is because you are not focusing on the edge alone but on the entire blade.
- Your technique involves a process similar to the hollow grind. Bring the edge close to the grinding wheel or belt.
- When the edge is sharp, continue working on the blade towards the spine.
- Once you are done, you should notice a linear slope that starts from the edge and goes all the way to the spine.

## The Convex Grind

A convex edge is where the blade has a bevel on each side that is slightly curved. Convex edges are said to be rather difficult to accomplish by hand. The ideal way to work on these grinds is by using a belt grinder. Here is how you can create this grind on your knife.

- For convex edges, we are first going to make sure that we leave off a little bit of thickness on the edge because we do not want it to get too thin.
- You want to start off by first flat-grinding the edge.
- Once you have completed the flat grind, you should then use a 60 grit belt on the grinder. You need to hold the knife at a slight angle, but not too much because you need the sides of the blade to touch the belt.

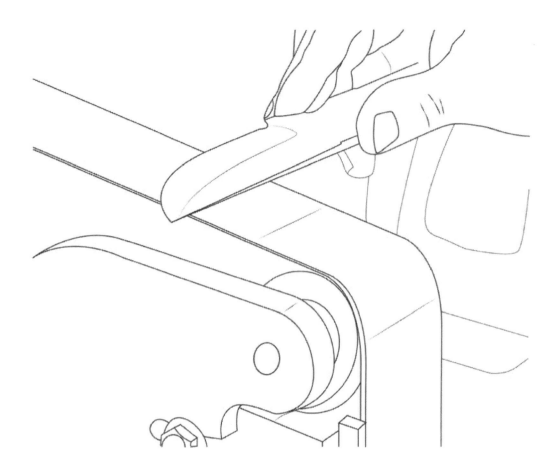

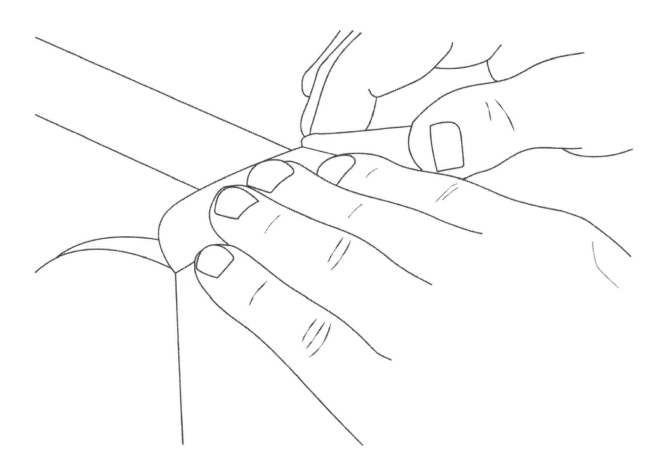

Figure 16 & 17: Grinding on top of the belt sander helps

- With that angle, bring the side of the blade to the belt and then start grinding.
- While grinding, you need to move the knife back and forth a little bit along the edge. Start doing this on one side and then flip the knife over. Continue grinding the knife on the other side at an angle.
- Flip the knife over every two rotations of the grind.
- Once you have completed the grind, you now have a convex shape along the side of the knife.
- Now we focus on the edge. Touch the edge lightly to the belt. Don't press down too much on it.
- Move the knife and allow the belt to form a nice convex edge.
- Flip the knife over and work on the edge from the other side.
- Eventually, you are going to achieve a nice convex edge.

## Tips for Grinding

- Always remember to use your hips instead of your wrist while shifting grind lines. Aim to keep your elbows close to your sides, your shoulders back and your stomach tight. All of these simple adjustments will allow you to have better control over your grinding process.
- Be confident near the grinder. Keep your movements controlled and stable. As we had already seen, do not try to press against the grinder too hard.

## How Thin Should The Edge Be?

Here is a common question that many knifemakers come across: how thin or thick should the knife-edge be? What you should look for is the purpose of the knife.

The general rule of thumb is that thicker blades are used to cut harder materials. You might use them for cutting wood or skinning game. On the other hand, a thinner knife is used for slicing, like the kitchen knives.

So how thick or thin should your knife edge be? Well, if you are using it for hunting purposes, then you should make it about 1.5mm thick. If you intend to slice through things and need the right sharpness for it, then your knife edge should be about 0.3mm.

# Chapter 6: Heat Treating

Essentially, no material or finished product can be manufactured without sending it through the process of heat treating. In this process, a particular metal is heated to a high temperature and then cooled under specific conditions to improve its characteristics, stability, and performance.

Through heat treatment, you can soften a metal, which allows the metal to become more flexible. You can also use heat treatment to harden metals, ensuring that their strength is improved.

Heat treatment is essential if you are in the business of manufacturing parts for automobiles, aircrafts, computers, heavy machinery, and tools. In other words, if you want something important built, then you need to subject the material to heat treatment.

Iron, and more specifically, steel, are the most common materials that go through heat treatment. However, that does not mean that other materials cannot be treated with heat. By other materials, we mean your knife.

In short, this process is quite important, and you are going to learn to use it. But more importantly, let us look at each process and try to understand what it means.

## Tempering

One of the processes of heat treatment is called tempering. In this process, you are basically altering the mechanical attributes (usually the flexibility and strength) of steel or products and items made from steel. Tempering releases the carbon molecules confined in the steel to diffuse from martensite. Martensite is a form of a crystalline structure consisting of brittle carbon that exists in hardened steel. Because of martensite's features, the steel may be hard, but it also becomes brittle, rendering it useless in most applications.

Tempering allows the internal stresses that may have been formed due to past uses to be discharged from the steel. This results in the alloy becoming more durable.

So how does one temper their steel? Firstly, the steel is heated to a high temperature, but it is not allowed to heat up beyond its melting point. Once that is done, it is then cooled in air. There is no fixed temperature for all forms of steel. They each have their own temperature range that must be reached first.

When you temper the steel, it is important to heat it gradually until it reaches the temperature you would like to work with. This prevents the metal from cracking.

## Annealing

Annealing is another process of heat treatment, focused on softening the steel or reducing the hardness of the material. This is done so that it is easier to machine the steel.

In this process, the metal is heated to a temperate where it is possible to attain re-crystallization. This means that new non-deformed grains take over the positions of the deformed grains. And what exactly are grains? In metallurgy, each grain is a single crystal that consists of a specific arrangement of atoms. When you have deformed grains, then you cannot work on the metal without causing more deformity. In this case, the deformity appears in the form of cracks. When you perform the annealing process, you are forming new grains, which means you are allowing yourself to work on the metal again.

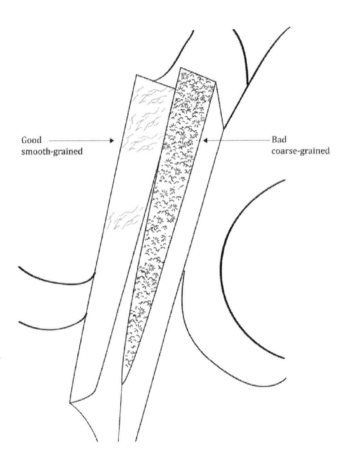

Figure 18: Good Grain vs Bad Grain

## Normalizing

During normalizing, you are refining the size of the grain in the metal. After normalizing, the mechanical properties of the metal are improved.

Normalizing sets a uniformity to the structure of grains in the metal. After you have achieved uniformity, you have reduced the degree of deformity of the metal. This allows you to get a smooth finish and a wonderful product in the end.

Normalizing is usually used to remove the stresses built up inside a piece of steel and bring it back to its initial state.

In the process of normalizing, steel is heated to a high temperature and then cooled by leaving the metal at room temperature. This process of rapidly heating the metal and then slowly cooling it down makes changes in the microstructure of the alloy, making it elastic and durable. Normalizing is almost like a process of correction. This is because it is typically used when some other process unintentionally increases the hardness but decreases the malleability of the metal. What makes normalizing different from other methods such as annealing is that it uses room temperature to cool down the metal, rather than any medium or special technique.

## Heat Treatment for 1084 and 1085 steel

1084 has a somewhat higher manganese composition than other carbon steels in the 10XX category. Because it is a relatively easy steel to work with, it makes 1084 an ideal steel for beginners who want to start their bladesmithing adventure. It gives you enough room to make errors when it comes to heat treatment. It is known to form an almost complete 'pearlite' structure when you subject it to annealing and normalizing processes. Pearlite is a structure that features alternating layers.

Additionally, 1084 contains nearly 0.84% carbon (which is represented by the 84 in 1084) and is known to produce a good quality knife with a nice edge. Below is the full working sequence for 1084 steel.

1085 steel has a somewhat higher manganese composition than other carbon steels in the 10XX category.

It's awfully similar to 1084 steel.

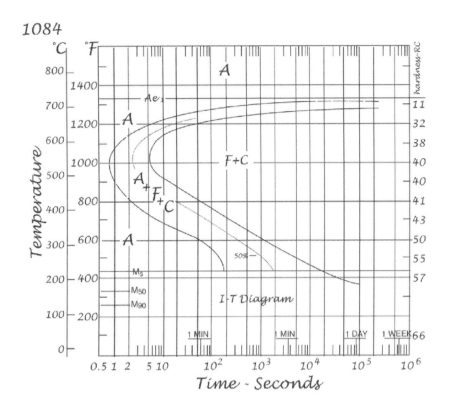

Figure 19: TTT graph of 1084 steel (It's the same for 1085 steel)

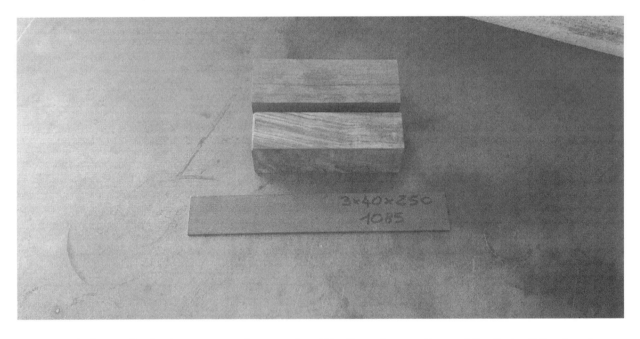

Because it is a relatively easy steel to work with, it makes 1085 an ideal steel for beginners who want to start their bladesmithing adventure.

It gives you enough room to make errors when it comes to heat treatment.

Following is the full working sequence for 1085 steel.

## Forging (Ignore if you did stock removal)

You start by forging using the steps mentioned in Chapter 4. Once you have forged the knife, you can then move on to the heat treatment, beginning with the annealing process.

## Hardening

**Step 1:** For this, you heat the steel to 1500°F.

Or you can aim to push it past its non-magnetic limit. In this case, that limit is around 1425°F.

As you heat it, keep checking if it's turned non-magnetic.

When you have reached such a state, you heat it to a slightly higher temperature. This is just to make sure that you have truly pushed the steel into the non-magnetic area.

If you overheat the steel by keeping it at temperatures of 1550°F or beyond and you quench the metal, the metal could form grains.

## Quenching

1085 doesn't need a fast-quenching oil. You can use canola oil for quenching 1085.

Preheat the canola oil to about 135°F. Once done, quench the metal for about 10-15 seconds.

To make sure the blade has hardened, we can do a file test.

## Tempering

If you have been following the instructions, then your steel should be around 65RC. At this level, it is fairly fragile, so do not drop it. It might shatter upon hitting the ground.

| Tempering Temperature | | Rockwell Hardness |
|---|---|---|
| ºC | ºF | HRC |
| 149 | 300 | 65 |
| 177 | 350 | 63-64 |
| 204 | 400 | 60-61 |
| 232 | 450 | 57-58 |
| 260 | 500 | 55-56 |
| 288 | 550 | 53-54 |
| 316 | 600 | 52-53 |
| 343 | 650 | 50 |

Rockwell Hardness Scale for 1085 steel

We need to bring the hardness of the steel down to about 59 HRC.

Bring the steel to room temperature and begin tempering it once it reaches that temperature. Heat the steel to a little bit above 400°F. Temper twice.

Each tempering process should be done for two hours. Allow the steel to return to room temperature between the two processes.

Ideally, your method should follow this sequence: temper for two hours, then return to room temperature, and then back to tempering.

And that's it! Your blade is now heat treated.

# Heat Treatment for 1095 steel

Working with 1095 steel is pretty simple. It is a steel with a high carbon content, and you can use it to forge shapes easily. It does have lower traces of manganese than other steel that are part of the 10XX series (such as the 1080 steel.) However, the comparatively higher rate of carbon means that it provides more carbide that can be used for providing resistance to abrasions. However, this also means that because of the extra carbon, you might have to put in more care during the heat treatment.

If you are going to heat treat 1095 steel, I would suggest that you have a temperature-controlled forge.

But let's go through all the steps in the process so that you can understand what is happening. Given below is the total working sequence for 1095 steel.

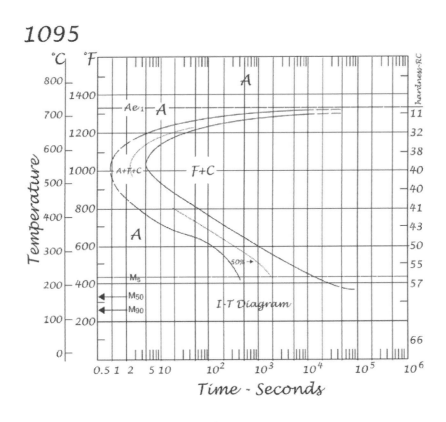

Figure 20: TTT graph of 1095 steel

## Forging

We first start with the forging process. Take 1095 through the forging process that was mentioned earlier.

## Normalizing

To normalize the steel, you have to bring the temperature of the metal to 1575°F. Let the metal sit inside the forge at that precise temperature, for 5 minutes. Once the 5 minutes are over, allow the metal to cool in the air till it reaches room temperature.

Another way to normalize is a little bit tricky. Get to 1575°F and choke your forge so it spits flames out of the opening and turn down the gas. It should maintain the same color inside as it did when you reached 1575°F.

## Annealing

For the annealing process, you start by heating the metal to 1475°F. Cooling should be at a rate no faster than 50°F per hour.

The easiest way to cool the steel is by placing the blade inside a container of insulating, fireproof material. Wood ash is easily obtainable and a great insulator. Another option frequently used by knifemakers is vermiculite. Vermiculite is a mineral often used in gardening and can be found at any store that sells gardening supplies.

You could also go with the suggestion to cool it overnight. You have to keep the metal inside the forge to ensure the cooling is complete.

At this point, you can perform your machining or grinding process.

## Grinding and Machining the Steel

You can use any of the grinding techniques that were mentioned in the previous chapter at this point.

## Hardening

Heat to 1475°F which is the non-magnetic level of the knife. You can also heat just past that temperature, but ideally, stick to not going beyond that temperature. As explained before, this non-magnetic range of the temperature means that a magnet doesn't stick to the metal. Do not overheat the steel beyond 1550°F range. After heating move on to the quenching process.

## Quenching

1095 steel requires a fast quenching oil. For this reason, the safest option that you can pick for 1095 steel is a special quenching oil. One of the more common oils in the market that I recommend is the Parks 50 quench oil. Parks 50 is a fast quench and is almost as fast as water. For this reason, make sure you don't grind your knife too thin before heat treatment. You start off by first preheating the oil to 70-120°F. Put the blade into the oil for about 7-9 seconds, until you notice that the hissing and bubbling subsides. Once done, take out the knife from the oil. You can also make use of quenching oil manufactured by Maxim Oil.

Finally, you can use canola oil, but that's only if you can't procure Parks 50. I only recommend using it on thin 1095 stock, up to about 1/8 inch. You could do it for ¼ inch stock, but I haven't done it personally, so I can't tell you how well it'd work.

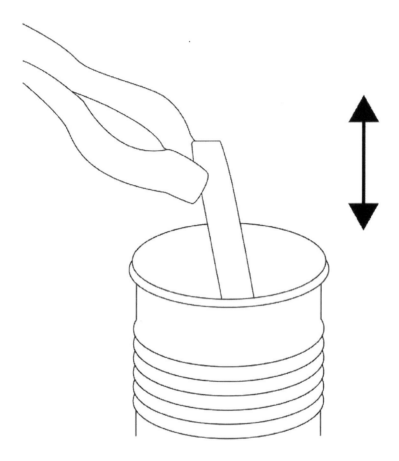

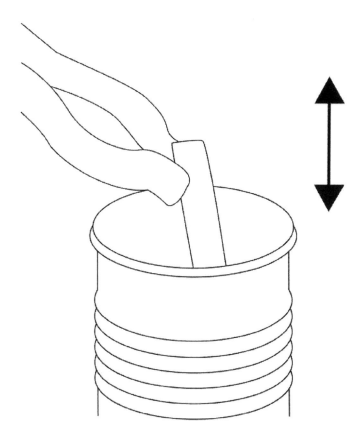

Figure 21 & 22: The dipping motion while quenching

When it comes to canola oil, preheat the oil to 135°F. Quench the knife in the liquid for about 10-15 seconds.

## Tempering

The tempering process for 1095 steel is simple. Place the steel in an oven, and heat the steel to 500°F. We are trying to achieve about 59-60 HRC.

This will allow the knife to have good performance in most situations. However, I would still not recommend that you drop it. You might not destroy it entirely, but you might cause cracks to appear. Temper it twice for two hours each. Make sure that you are allowing it to cool. Bring it down to room temperature before you temper it again.

## Cryo Treatment

Now, this step is not entirely necessary. However, it will improve the quality of the steel you are working with. If you like, you can skip this step altogether.

Soak the steel in temperatures ranging from -90°F to -290°F. The medium you should choose for cryo treatment should be liquid nitrogen. You need to ensure that you have introduced the metal to cryo treatment for about eight hours. For this, you can even soak the metal in liquid nitrogen overnight.

## Eliminating Blemishes, Scaling, and Warps After Heat Treatment

### *By Hand*

**Step 1:** Start with 320 grit sandpaper. We cross the oblique pass and straight pass over each other.

First sand it in an oblique motion.

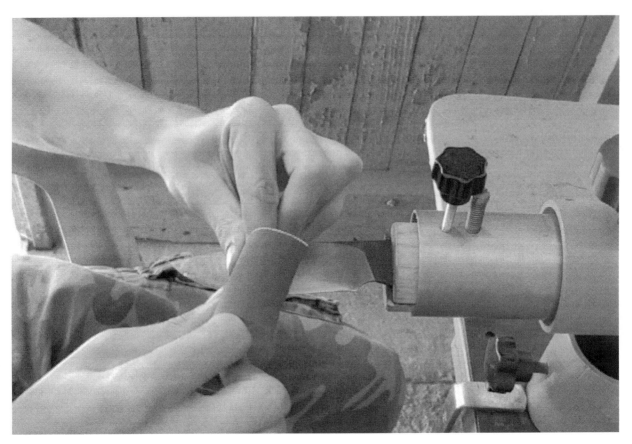

Then cross in a straight motion.

**Step 2:** When the blade becomes smooth and all the scratches look the same, replace them with finer scratches using 600 grit sandpaper.

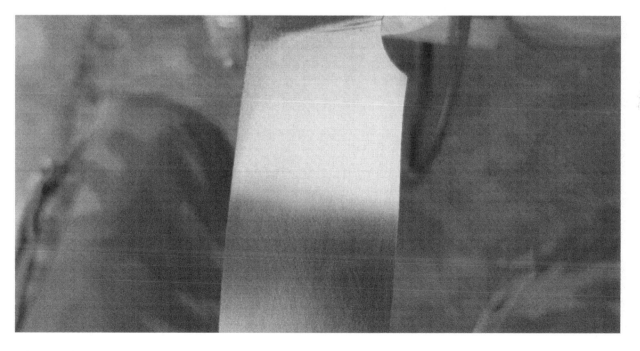

That is the basic principle behind sanding your knife, replacing bigger scratches with smaller ones until they're too small to notice.

**Step 3:** When all the scratches become homogenous using the 600 grit sandpaper, instead of doing oblique or straight passes, do vertical passes to have a final effect with all the lines running through the blade.

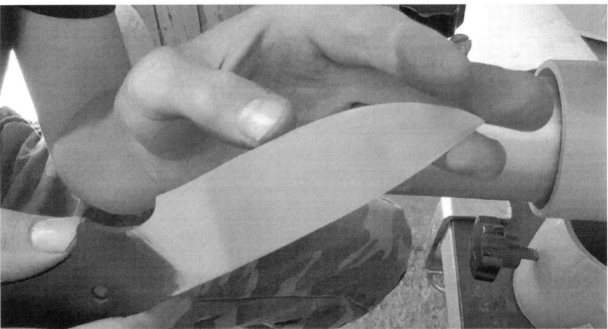

**Step 4:** The blade is now properly hand sanded. We move on to sanding the tang. Since the tang will be hidden by the handle, you don't need to be too meticulous.

## *Using a Belt Sander*

At this point, it is especially important not to let your blade get hot on the grinder and ruin the heat treatment. Have a water drum near the grinder and dip the steel frequently. This way, if you feel that the knife is getting too hot, you can immediately dip it in the water to cool it.

But this time, there is a slight difference in how you approach the grinder. Usually, you hold the knife out horizontally and then grind away any of the materials still on the knife. This time, however, you are going to hold the knife vertically and then grind away.

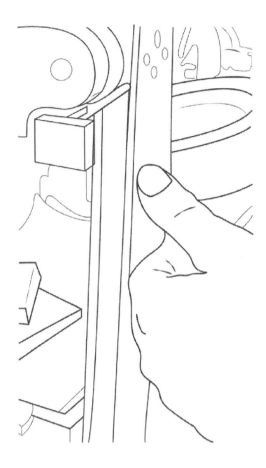

Figure 23: Vertical sanding is very effective in removing blemishes

One of the things that you will notice is that the sanding process might not remove some of the marks near the ricasso area.

For this, do not head back to the grinder again. If you can, take out the belt and use it manually to remove the blemishes and scaling. What you can do is use a long wooden stick. Tack one end of the belt onto one end of the wooden stick and the other end of the belt on the opposite end of the stick.

Bring the improvised belt to the knife and slowly sand away the remaining blemishes that you see.

## Truing Your Knife

While most people assume that handheld blades are perfectly straight, the sad reality is that most blades are not straight. In fact, not only are most blades bent, but many are twisted as well.

So why are so many blades far from being straight? The answer lies in the fact that most people, knifemakers included, have not been taught to examine blades carefully.

Why is examining the blade important? This is because when you examine the blade, you get to check it for any defects or anomalies that you might have missed out earlier. Typically, when your blade is warped, then you might notice it easily. However, sometimes, you might have to check to make sure if there is a bend in your knife, especially when it might not be clear if there even exists a bend or not.

Here is how you do it.

Now we are going to use the idea of your dominant eye and non-dominant eye. Your dominant eye is the one you use to examine something. For example, if you want to peek at an object, then you often close one eye and open wide the other. The open eye is your dominant eye.

Let us start with the knife diagnosis.

To diagnose the straightness of a blade, hold the blade in such a way that the handle is furthest away from you. The edge of the knife should be towards the ground and the point aimed at your dominant eye. The non-dominant eye is closed. The back, or spine, of the knife should be in full view. Not only can the spine be examined for straightness this way, but straightness from the blade continuing to the end of the handle can be examined. Some blades are reasonably straight, only to slightly bend off somewhere along their bodies. Most will be bent one way or the other.

Sometimes, when you subject your knife to the heat treatment process, you might notice that it warps.

Warping happens for many reasons. Here are some of the causes for it:

- Heat treating of the blade is a delicate process. When you are subjecting it to all that heat, you might have to be careful how you distribute that heat. Sometimes, when bladesmiths use coal forge, they often forget to plunge the knife into the coal rather than simply place it on top of the distributed coals.
- During grinding, if cracks and splits are still present on the knife, then this can cause heated to be concentrated in certain areas, eventually causing the blade to warp.
- Make sure that you haven't skipped the tempering process or, for that matter, any process mentioned in the heat treatment of the blade. Remember that the only optional treatment is the cryo treatment. Everything else is important and should be followed in the steps mentioned above.
- Try and bring your metals as close to the non-magnetic limit as possible. This allows you to work with the metal better.
- Don't quench your knife in a sideways motion. Doing so will increase the chances of warping your knife.

Now let us assume that you have a warped knife. What can you do in this case? How can you straighten out the metal?

The process is fairly simple.

The first thing that you have to do is heat up the knife along the convex side of the curve. Once that is done, you can then hammer the knife or untwist it (or you can do both).

Let's look at each process.

Hammering

- When you are hammering, try to use the weight of your hammer to your advantage. If you find yourself holding on to your hammer with white knuckles, figure out how to get more comfortable.
- Find a rhythm and swing with your hammer instead of fighting against it. You can continue to hammer until you see the knife being straightened out. The index finger of the support hand is held at the exact spot to locate the problem. The blade is lowered to the anvil or your workbench, the convex side of the bend facing up, without removing the fingertip from the blade.
- A quick visual check confirms the exact spot on the blade where the hammer will strike. As the dominant hand reaches for the hammer, the support hand breaks contact with the blade to hold the blade by the handle in preparation for the coming hammer blow.
- A more forceful blow follows one very light strike to confirm the accuracy of the technique.

The blade is reexamined for results and repeated if necessary. In this technique, the emphasis is on proper diagnosis rather than on hammering technique.

Untwisting

- You can also untwist the knife. The best way to accomplish this is by using clamps to hold the knife properly while you use the tongs to straighten the knife. This process works to remove the warp easily, but it might require more strength from your end.
- Another way you can untwist the knife is by holding the knife in a vise. You have to make sure that the portion of the blade that has incurred the bend is placed in the center of the vise (since that is the part that is going to get twisted). Clamp down on the vise as tightly as possible, this will put pressure on the knife, and begin to straighten.
- If the twist is too small for your hammer, then you can make use of a metal rod. Make sure that the rod is thin enough to work with the twist that you have. Place the knife between a vise and clamp it hard. Once you have done that, position the rod so that it is aimed at the twist. Using your hammer, strike the rod softly until you can untwist the knife.

# Chapter 7: Handle

**Note:** This guide is very detailed. Since this is meant for beginners, we wanted to make sure there is very little room for error for you guys :)

To make the handle for your blade, you will attach two pieces of material to the outside of your tang. These pieces are called scales. You can make your scales out of a wide variety of natural and man-made materials.

While there are some benefits and drawbacks of using certain materials, a lot of this comes down to personal preference. When choosing the material for a knife handle, you should take into consideration the environment and the kind of abuse your handle will need to take. If you're going to be hammering on your handle frequently during the process of batoning, it might not make sense to use a softwood that could be easily damaged. Changes in temperature and humidity will also make some natural materials shrink and swell, which could affect the integrity of your handle.

**TIP**: Using a bolster will shorten the length of handle scales that you will need for your handle. Take account of that when making the handle design.

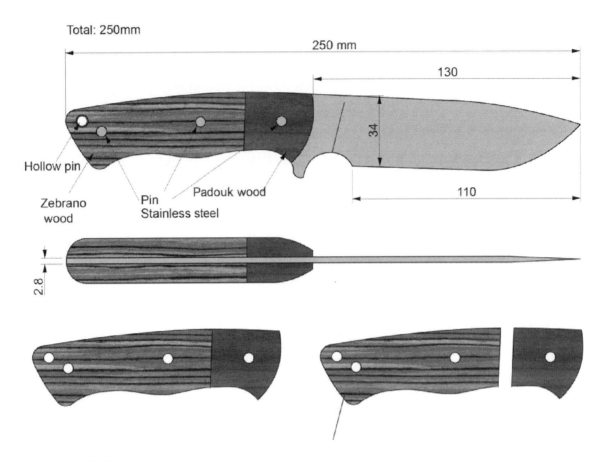

## Scale Material

Along with wood, one of the recommended knife handles you can use is made out of Micarta scales. Micarta is a form of synthetic material that is made out of certain kinds of fabrics, such as linen or canvas. They are usually soaked in resin. It is tough, lightweight, and makes a durable handle. When the handle is exposed to an oily or greasy liquid, however, it will make the Micarta a bit slippery. But that is a small drawback for an otherwise suitable material.

Another thing that you need to focus on is the pins that will be inserted into the tang and the handle. Pins are the pieces of thin, round metal that are inserted through holes to help hold the scales to a full-tang blade. These pins, once finished, will leave a small circle of metal visible on the handle. Pins can be made out of almost any kind of metal, depending on what you would like to see on your handle.

I would also recommend using Corby fasteners and Loveless bolts, if you have the taste for them.

This project will have a composite handle made of zebran and padouk wood.

### Steps:

**Step 1:** We first begin with the bolster that we will make out of padouk wood.

94

Mark a line 13mm from the edge of the wood block and score it using a caliper.

Alternatively, you can simply mark the line with a scribe and a ruler.

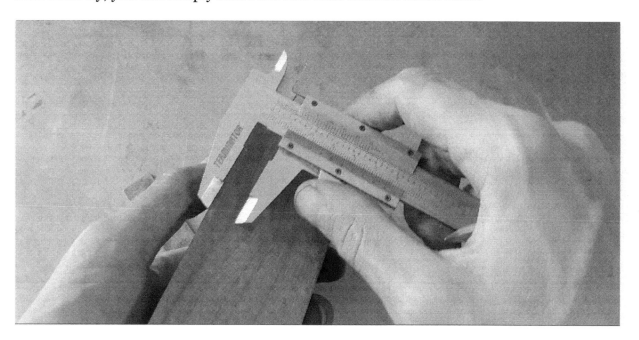

**Step 2:** Cut the wood block along that line using a bandsaw or a hacksaw.

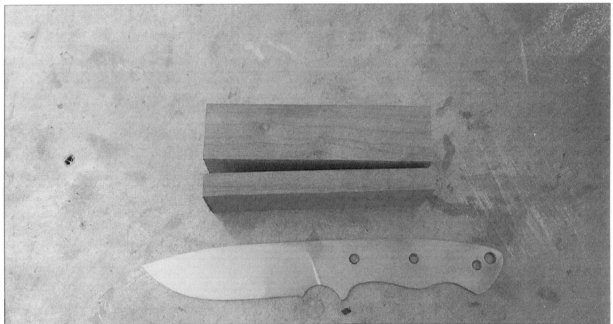

This 13mm thick strip of wood is be used to make the bolster.

**Step 3:** Repeat the same process for the zebran wood block twice. This will give us 2 13mm thick strips that will be our handle scales.

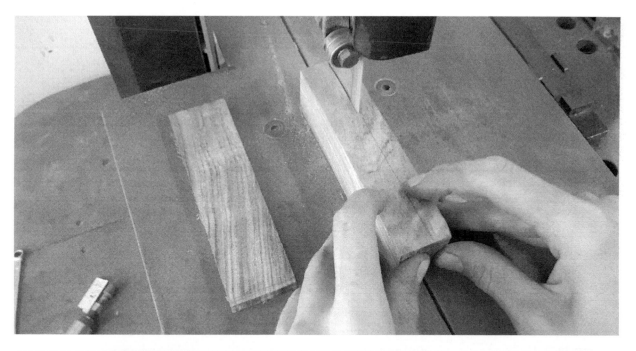

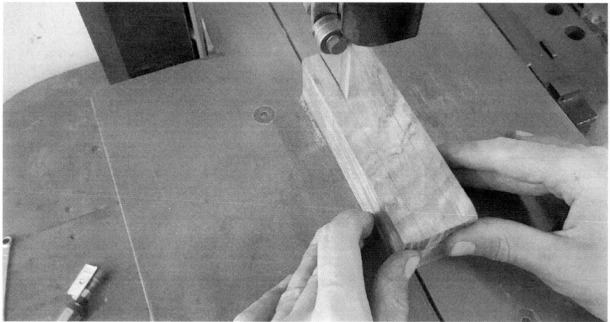

Doing Steps 1-3 will ensure you get maximum value out of every wood block you purchase.

**Step 4:** Split the padouk wood scale into two, to form either side of the bolster.

**Step 5:** Sand the scales and bolster to smooth out each area that will be glued using epoxy. This way they will sit flush with anything they are glued to.

A disc sander is used for this. But you can also use a belt grinder or 600 grit sandpaper to do anything that the disc sander does.

**Step 6:** Now it's time to put epoxy to attach the bolster and the scale.

Before you begin, mark the surfaces that will be glued using a pencil.

**Step 7:** For applying the epoxy you will need the following materials:

- Earbuds
- Epoxy (Resin and hardener)
- Tape
- Clamps (You can also use something heavy that you don't mind getting epoxy on)
- Baking paper

**TIP:** Place the scales over baking paper after you spread epoxy, because it does not stick to epoxy.

Once the epoxy has cured, the bond is very hard to break.

The baking paper will help prevent it from getting into your workbench or other areas of your workshop.

**Step 8:** Once you have all the materials ready, mix the resin and hardener in 1:1 ratio. Different epoxy brands may have different ratios, so read the instructions given in the packaging carefully.

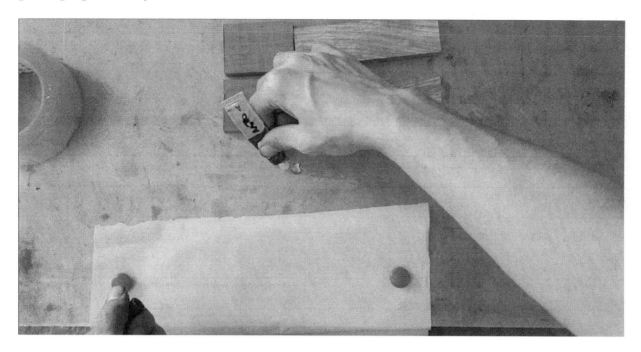

Apply the epoxy on the bolster surface where it will glued to the handle scale. Do the same for the handle scale.

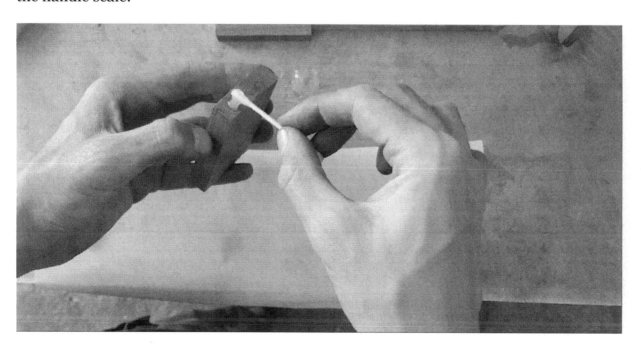

Attach them together and clamp them over baking paper.

**Step 9:** Once the epoxy has cured. Our handle scales are ready for grinding!

First, cut out the handle shape from the template.

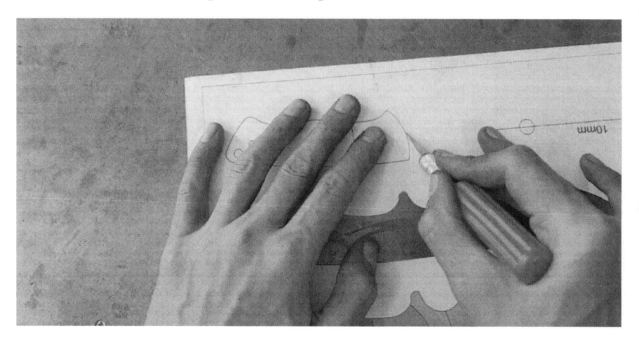

**Step 10:** Temporarily join the two scales together using double-sided tape.

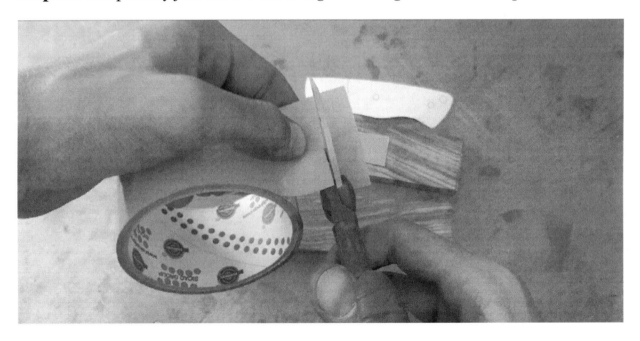

**Step 11:** With the line between the bolster and handle as reference, place the template onto the handle scale. Roughly mark the handle using a pencil.

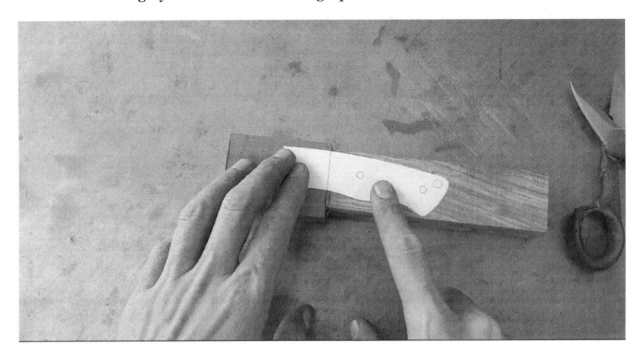

**Step 12:** Cut out the excess material using a bandsaw.

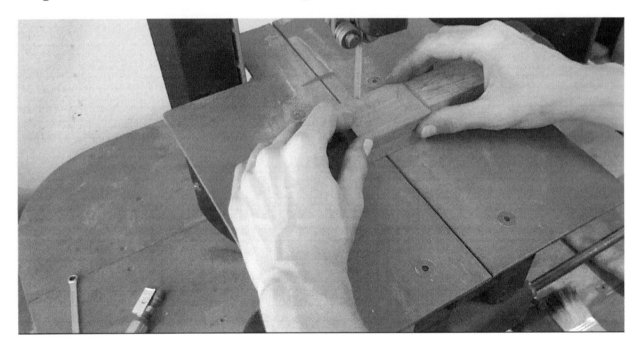

**Step 13:** Sand the surface of the handle until the thickness of the bolster scale and handle scale becomes equal.

You can alternatively use a hacksaw to roughly even out the thickness and then smooth it out with _____ grit sandpaper.

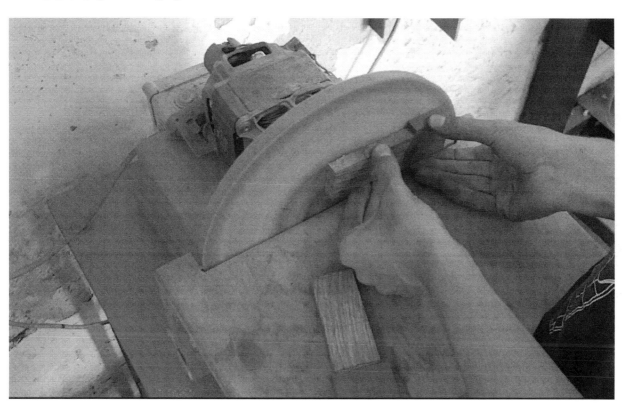

**Step 14:** Sand the handle scales with 600 grit paper so that they will sit flush when glued to the tang.

Sand the scales to form an '8' on the sandpaper. This will help ensure the surface of the scale is flat.

**Step 15:** Scribe the division between the bolster and the handle onto the blade.

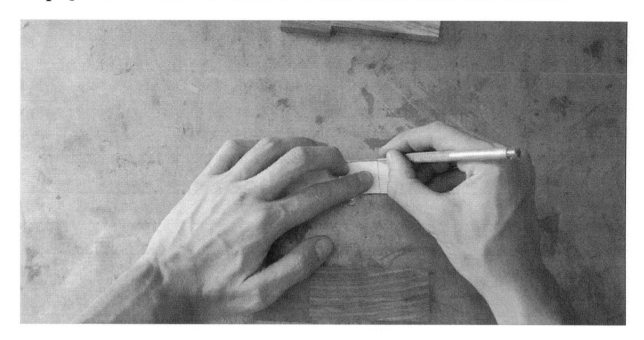

**Step 16:** Tape the tang of the blade with one of the handle scales.

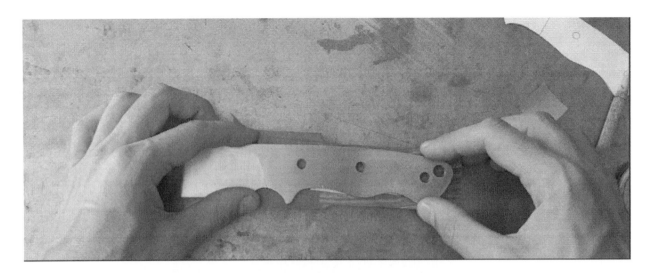

**Step 17:** Drill the pinholes into the handle scale.

**Step 18:** Detach the blade and couple the handle scales.

Drill the pinholes into the other handle scale.

Use the previous holes as a guide and gradually drill into the other scale.

Insert the pins or the correct sized drill bits (5mm for normal pins and 6mm for the hollow pin) into the holes.

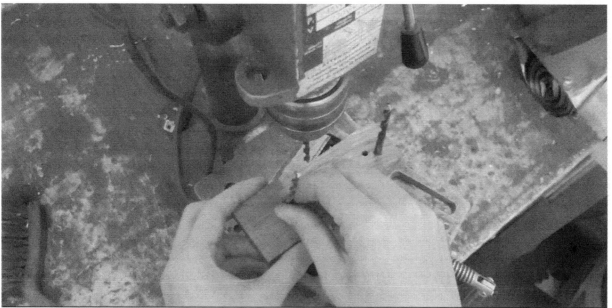

**Step 19:** Cut out the bolster from the template.

Using the inserted pins/drill bits as reference, we bring back the shape of the handle.

Put the bolster template through the bolster pin.

Mark the top of the bolster outline by pencil.

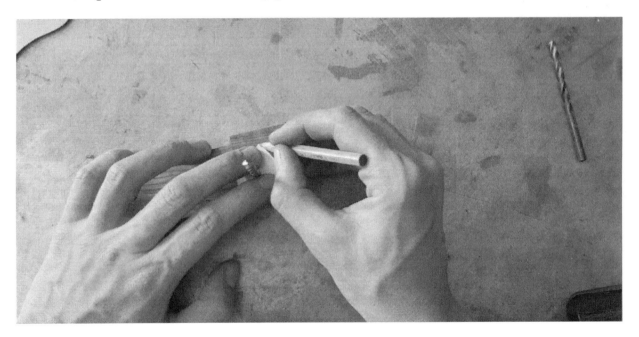

Roughly cut along the marking using a bandsaw.

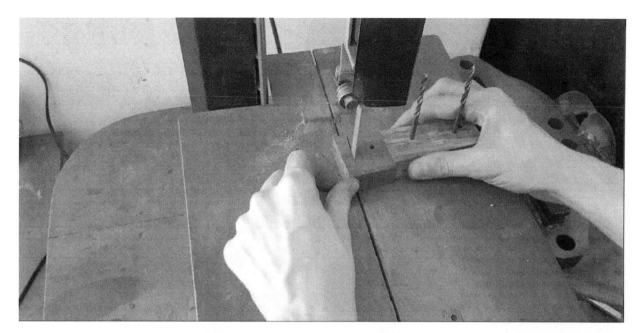

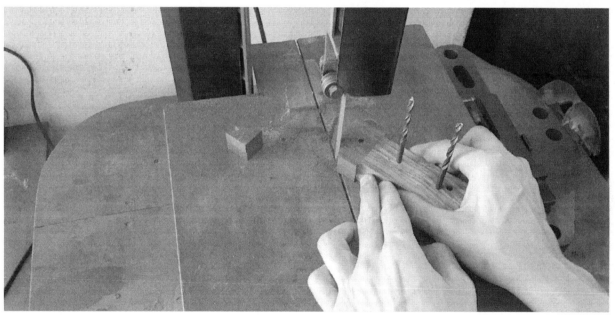

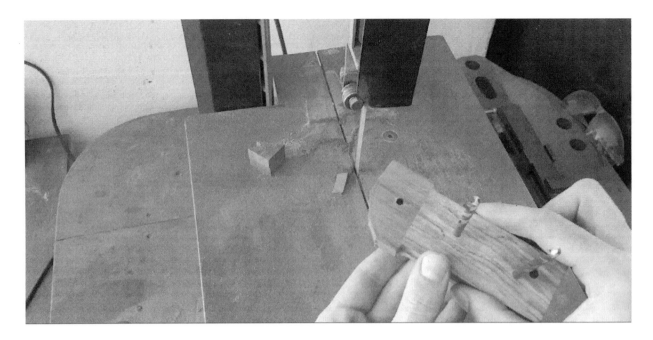

Smooth it out.

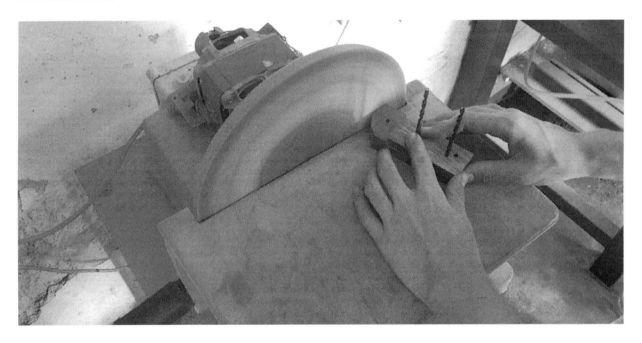

Repeat this step for the rest of the bolster and then the handle.

Finally you will end up with your handle scales looking like this.

**Step 20:** Mark the inside surfaces that will be glued to the tang using marker.

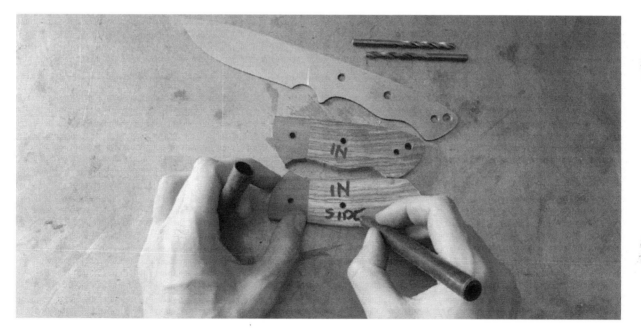

Mark the outline of the bolster 0.5 cm from the top, on both the scales.

**Step 21:** Tilt the disc sander like shown below.

Gradually run the top of the handle scales along the sander. Only do this for the outside (non-marked side) of the handle scales.

This will result in a gradual curve on the outside of the handle, that will soften the gap between the blade and handle.

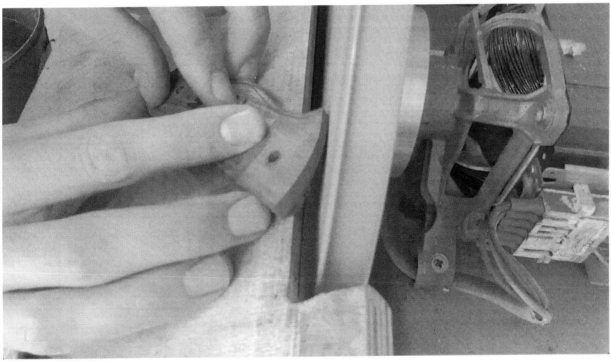

117

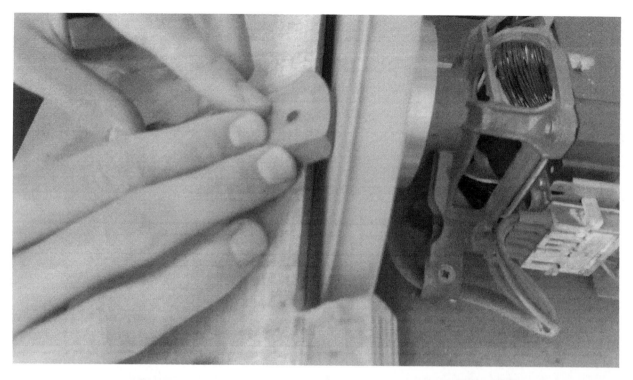

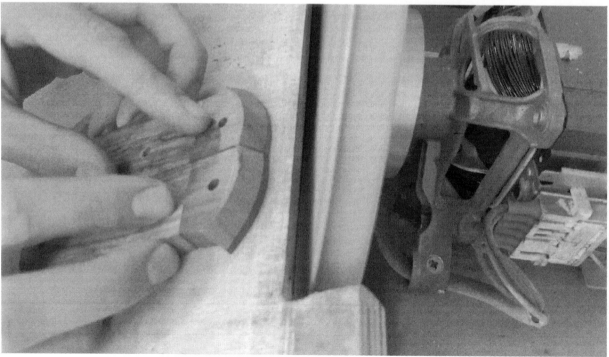

**Step 22:** Join the scales by inserting pins/5mm drill bits back into the holes and hold the handle using a vise.

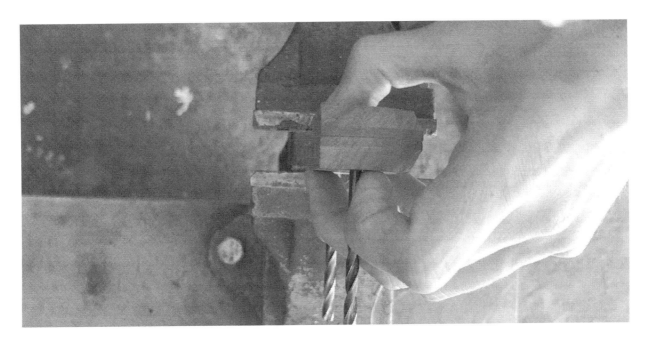

Hand sand the bolster using 800 grit sandpaper and make the curve smooth.

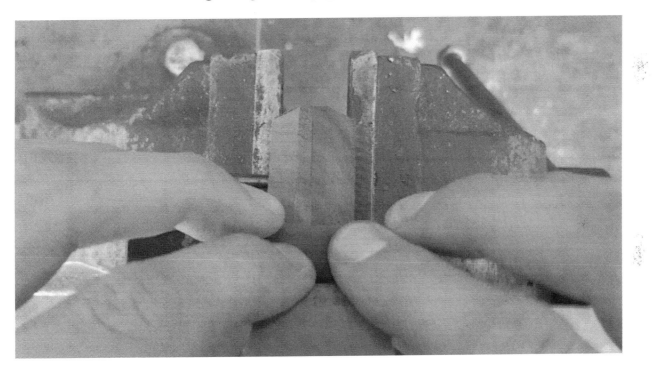

Finally it should something like this.

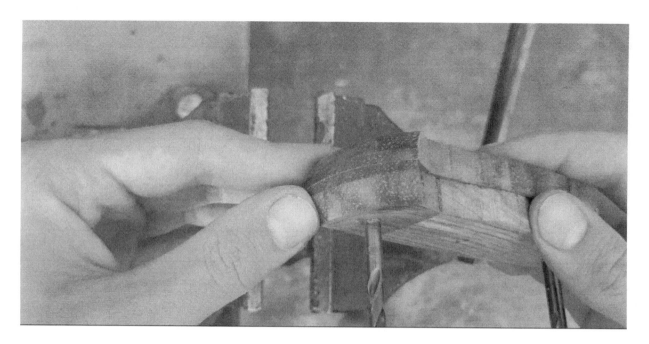

**Step 23:** Take the measurement for pin length, Length of pins = blade thickness + handle thickness + 0.5mm.

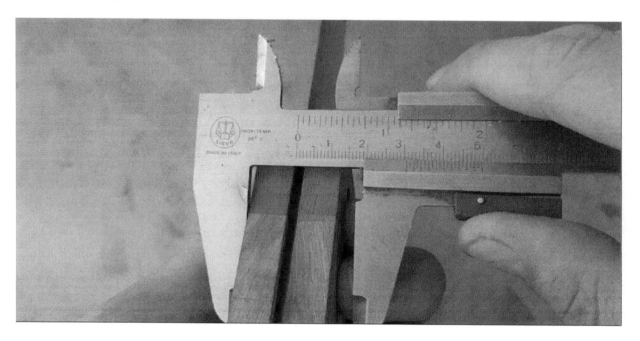

**Step 24:** Cut out the pins of the length we measure in the last step. For this project we need 3 5mm pins and 1 6mm hollow pin. Mark out the length using a marker.

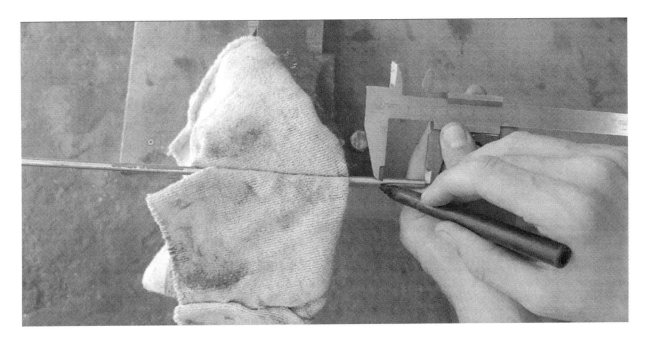

**TIP:** Wrap your vise with a rag, that will help it grip the pins better.

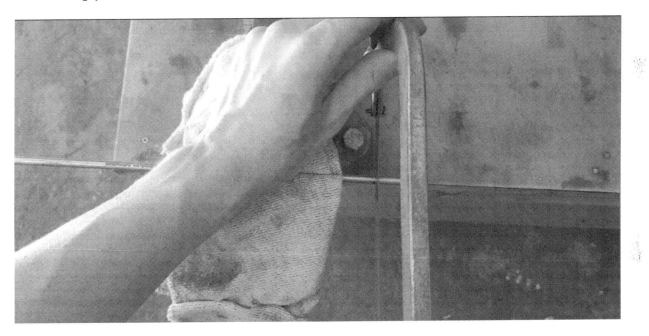

Smooth out the tips of the pins using a belt grinder/sandpaper.

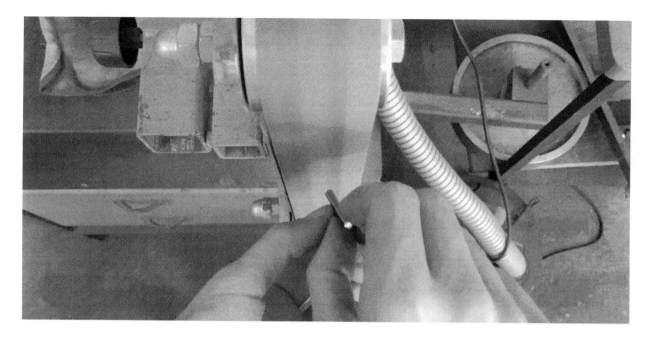

We are finally ready to apply epoxy and attach the scales to the tang.

**Step 25:** Mask off the blade using masking tape. This will ensure the epoxy does not get onto the blade. Place all the parts on baking paper.

Mix in the epoxy in the ratio mentioned in the packaging.

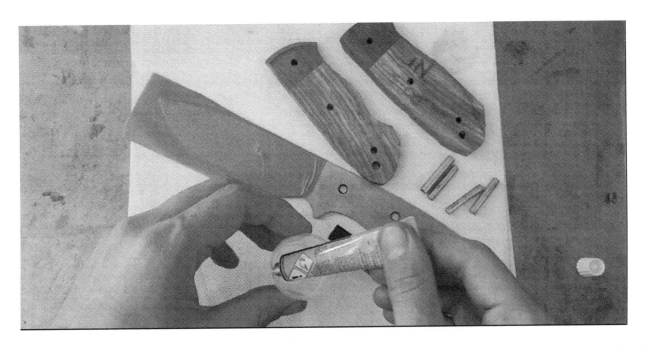

Start by applying epoxy inside the pin holes of one of the handle scales. Using an earbud will really help get the epoxy inside.

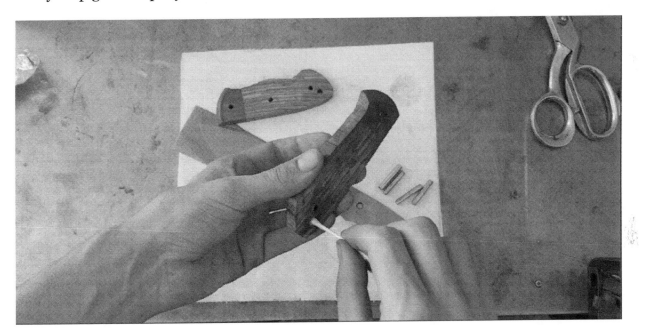

**Step 26:** Dip the tip of the pins in epoxy and tap them with a hammer into their respective pin holes.

**Step 27:** Apply epoxy to the inside of the handle scale and attach it to the tang.

Tap the pins with the hammer into the blade.

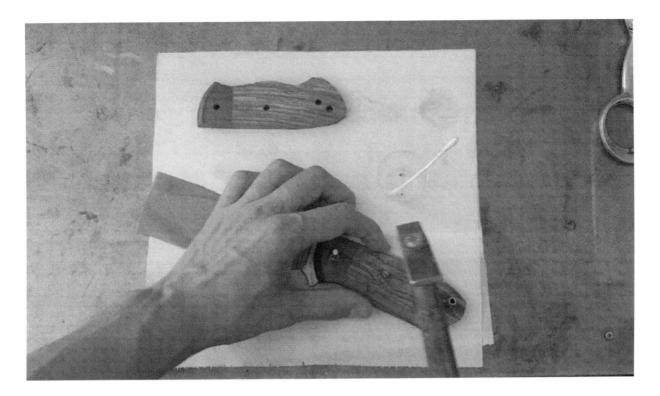

Now apply epoxy to the other handle scale and the exposed side of the tang.

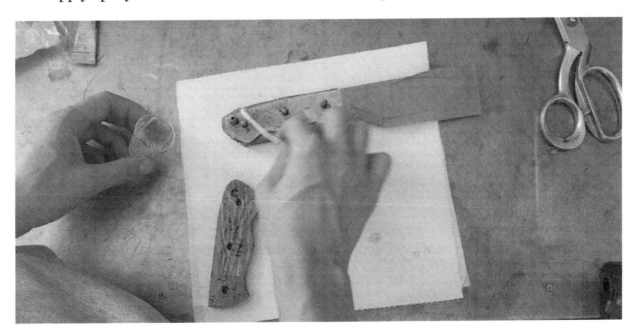

Hammer in the pins through the tang into the scale.

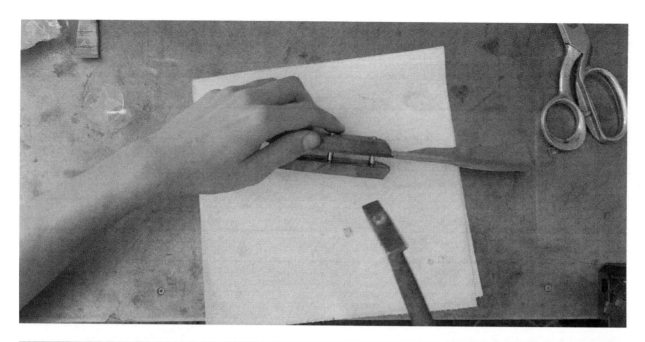

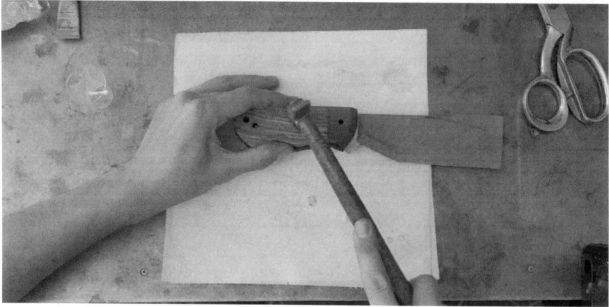

This process will take some time, and you will have go to back and forth between hammering either side of the handle, until the pins are fully inserted and the handle sits flush with the tang.

Once you are done, clamp the handle using two clamps and let the epoxy cure for 24 hours. Remove any excess glue that overflows with earbuds.

## Sanding and Shaping the Handle

**Step 1:** Grind either side of the handle, to smooth away the excess length of the pins on either side of the handle.

Don't press too hard. It may lead to overheating the pins and potentially burn up the epoxy, that will have no longer have any hold.

Just like while grinding the bevel, a light touch is all you need.

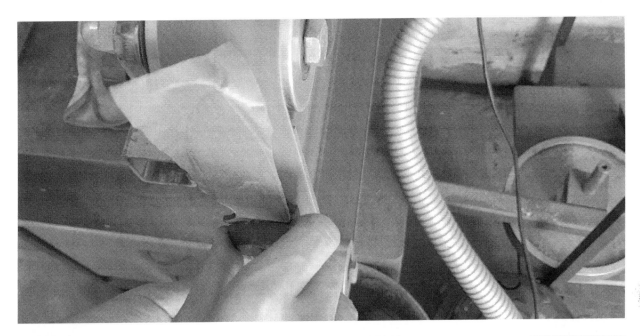

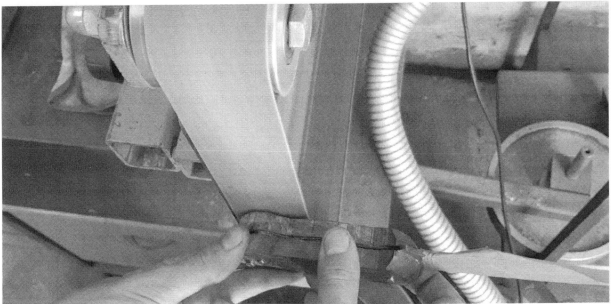

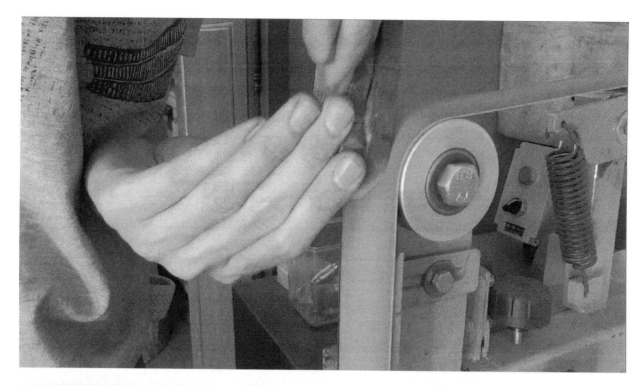

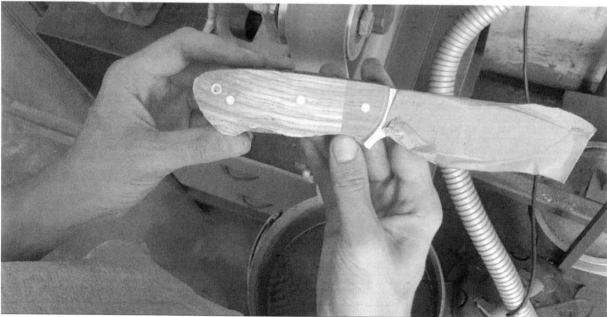

**Step 2:** Next we move to the front and spine of the handle.

Sand away the wood until you meet the steel, but go no further.

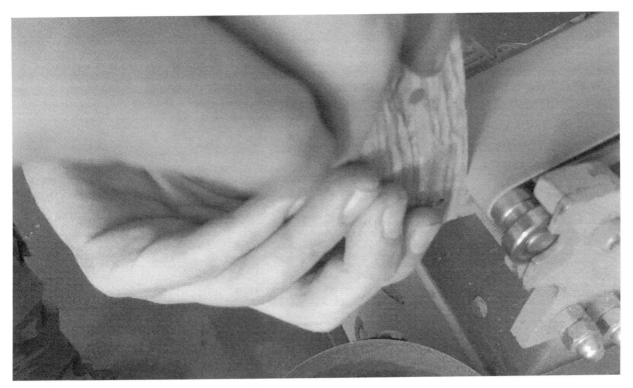

Continue across the perimeter of the handle until it looks like this:

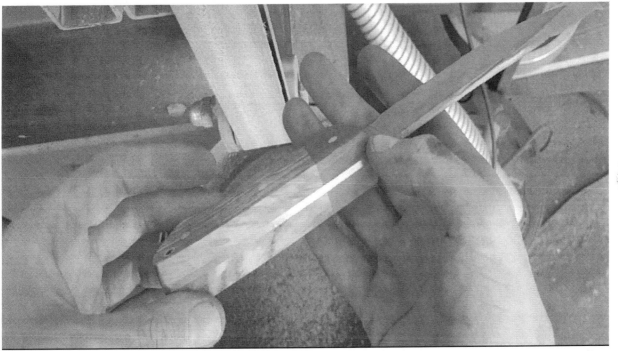

Let's move onto hand sanding the handle and rounding off it's edges to make it comfortable to hold.

## Hand Sanding the Handle

**Step 1:** Clamp down the blade.

Using 220 grit sandpaper, start rounding out the spine of the handle. Wrap the sandpaper around the spine and start sanding.

Once you're done with the spine, rip the sandpaper in half (lengthwise), and start sanding the front.

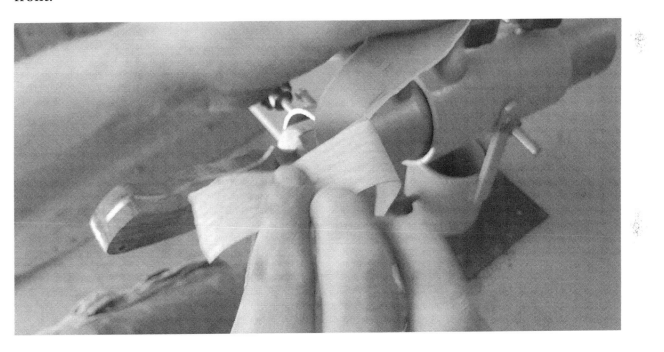

Rip off the sandpaper again (if it's getting dull use a new one) to sand curves of the front better.

Do this step till you're happy with how the handle feels.

**Step 2:** Apply linseed oil on the handle and blade as protective layer. This will also polish your handle.

Use your finger to rub it across the handle.

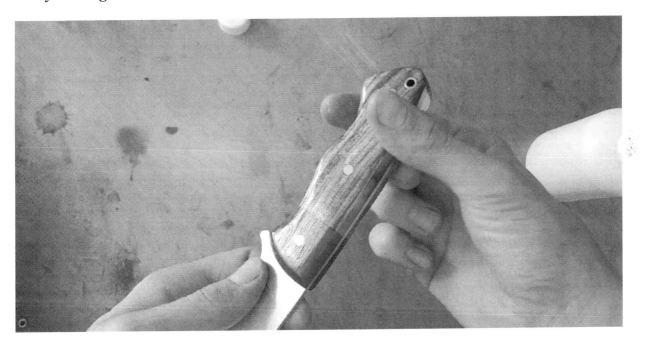

- A few things to remember during the sanding process:
  - Take a little extra time when you are sanding the pins. If you don't spend enough time, they might 'dome' out a bit. What this means is that they bulge out of their holes because the area around them is getting sanded faster than them.
  - Be careful when you are sanding near the areas that have metal. If you sand those

areas too much, then the metal will start protruding out, just like in the case with the pins.

○ After you have completed sanding using the 240 grit sandpaper, examine the handle and see if the results are according to your expectations. If you have to, redo the sanding process to get better results for your handle.

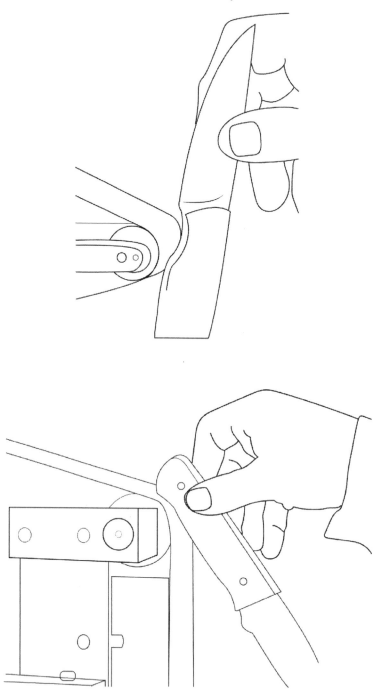

- Figure 31 & 32: A small wheel attachment on a 2X72 grinder can be handy in shaping the curves of the handle

# Chapter 8: The Final Processes

## Hand Satin Finishing for the Knife

- We had earlier worked on the handle, and this time, we are going to work on the blade. For finishing this knife, we are going to do a hand satin finish. We will basically replace deep scratches with finer ones, till the scratches are so fine that they aren't visible. If you want to sell your knife, then finishing it is necessary for your customer to feel good about his purchase.
- The best way to work with the knife is first clamping down a piece of board between a vise (make sure the board is narrow and more or less reaches the width of the knife blade). Then place the knife on top of the board and clamp the knife over there.
- Alternatively, cover the tang or handle of the knife with leather and then clamp the handle, leaving the blade projecting outward for you to work with your sandpaper.
- Use a little bit of WD40 and rub it along the blade. This elevates the sandpaper's cuts, and makes it last longer.
- Apply the WD40 on the belly of the knife. Whenever you are ready, take the sandpaper and place it on the blade that you are planning to finish. Then start moving the sandpaper along the length of the knife.
- You are going to sand the knife starting with an 80 grit sandpaper. Then continue using progressively higher grits as you remove scratches from the coarser sand paper.
- Remember that when you are using sandpaper, you want to work at an angle. Imagine the knife is pointed away from you. You start with the tip of the knife and move the sandpaper side-to-side as you make your way up the knife's blade, towards yourself.
- Rather than directly sanding the paper from left to right, you can adjust the sandpaper to be at an angle. So when you move from side-to-side, it looks like the sandpaper is positioned at a roughly 45° angle. This allows you to cover more surface area while you are sanding.
- Sand both sides of the knife using the above process. Once you have finished sanding, then you can work on the bevels. When you start working on the bevels, start by covering them with a blue marker. This allows you to check if there are any spots on the bevel. In case of spots, you should levelling should be done. Use a machined bar and dry paper to get the job done.
- Remember that the primary purpose of sanding is to remove any small scratch marks that might have appeared on the blade. In the end, when you have finished the sanding process, go over and check your work. Make sure that you are satisfied with the results. If you notice that there are still scratch marks, then take out the sandpaper and start working on it again.
- Don't be afraid to take time to remove the scratches. At this point, many knifemakers feel frustrated because they are so close to the end. They progress through the sanding process quickly to shoot through to the end. However, you should take your time. The fact that you are so close to finishing your knife might compel you to speed up the sanding process,

but you should take your time with it.
- Using a progression of grits for sanding will fetch you better results than jumping grit sizes.
- When you have done everything right, you should be left with a hand satin finish.

## Sharpening Your Knife

When you are working on the sharpening of your knife, you will come to realize that there are many sharpening tools out there in the market. Let us look at some of the tools that you can use for your sharpening process.

## Understanding More About Knife Sharpening

The thinness of an edge makes it the most vulnerable part of your knife. This is also the part of the blade that takes the most beating. Every knife requires edge maintenance eventually, as even the best steel wears with time. The basic mechanics of sharpening remain the same, whether it's your blade's first edge or its hundredth.

Some grinds do best with a small, secondary bevel on the very edge. Other grinds, such as the Scandi grind, are sharpened by refining the original grind. This makes the Scandi grind a very easy grind to sharpen for beginner, as the angle needed is easy to determine.

Make sure you have good lighting before you start the sharpening process. As with grinding, your sharpening process involves starting with coarse grit and slowly moving down to finer and finer grits.

When sharpening, the key is to match the angle of the knife's edge to the sharpener. By keeping this angle consistent and moving your edge across finer and finer grits, you'll remove all the metal that won't make up the edge of your blade. The mechanics behind sharpening aren't difficult to understand, but good results take a skilled hand and refined attention to detail.

## Knife Sharpening Techniques

### Technique 1: Using a Lansky System (Recommended for the beginner) Needs detailed steps

### Sharpening your Blade

We will be using a Lansky system to sharpen our blade.

The Lansky system is a beginner friendly way to sharpen your knives, without spending a lot of money on multiple sharpening stones.

### For this knife we will be sharpening at a 25-degree angle.

**Note:** This is not an advertisement for their product.

It's just what we think is the best option for a beginner who doesn't have a set of sharpening stones.

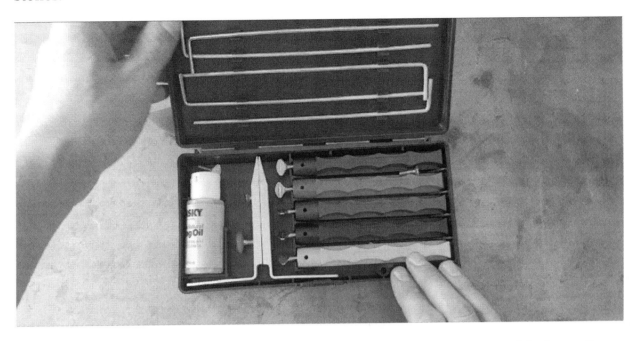

You can check out full instructions to use it in the 'Instructions' section of their product page at https://lansky.com/index.php/products/universal-system/

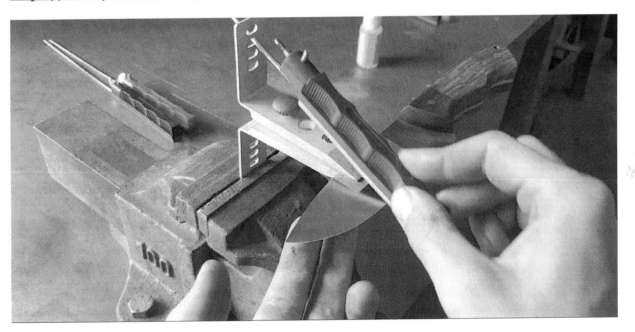

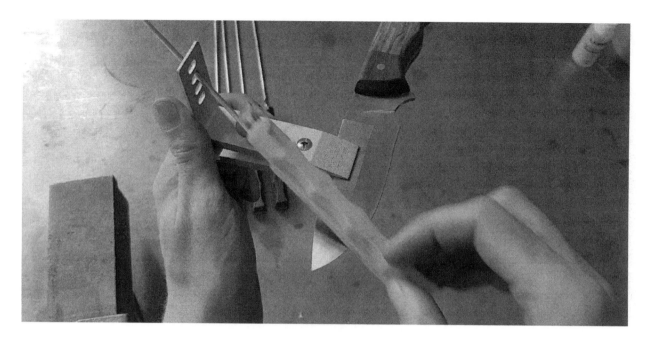

Once you're done sharpening, clean up the blade.

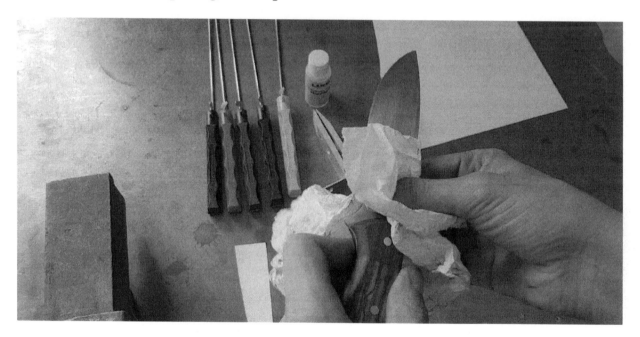

And that's it, you're knife build is complete.

## Technique 2: Using a Sharpening Stone (Recommended for the more experienced knifemakers)

- Hold your knife flat on its side on your coarse stone. Lift the spine slightly so that the edge is resting on the stone at a sharp angle. Ideally, you should keep an angle of about 20-25°. However, you can choose the angle that works best for your knife.

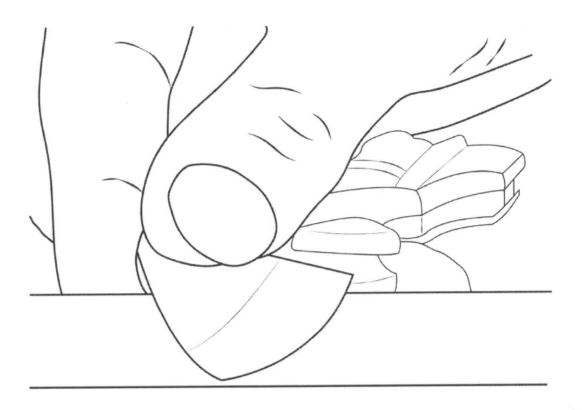

Figure 33: The correct sharpening angle

- Additionally, try and use a 1,000 grit stone in the beginning. This stone works well for beginners.
- Move the edge across the stone lightly, as if you were trying to slice off a very thin piece of it. Make sure the entire length of the blade, from the heel to the tip, comes in contact with the stone. Always sharpen your blade in the direction away from you. Repeat this process several times, maintaining the same angle.
- As you remove steel from the edge, a tiny burr will eventually form on the opposite side of the edge. The burr is a rough, raised metal curl that results from grinding metal. The burr should appear evenly along the entire length of the edge. If you find that it is absent in an area on your edge, you aren't sharpening as much on that particular spot.
- Once you have a burr along the entire edge, switch sides. Repeat the process until you have a burr on the second side. If you have any chips in your blade, you'll have to continue grinding with a coarse stone until all the steel is removed past that chip. Once you have set your edge with the coarse stone, move to a finer grit stone and repeat the whole process.
- Use a 'strop' method to remove the final burr on the blade's edge. Stropping involves the same motion that is used while sharpening on stone, but in reverse. Instead of cutting forward, the blade is drawn back, dragging the edge. Use light pressure and make several passes, alternating sides. Stropping makes sure that the sharpness of your blade remains

for a long time. Note that stropping stones are different from sharpening stones, and you should invest in one if you are serious about knifemaking.

**TIP:** Here is an important tip to remember while sharpening your knife. Make sure that you clean your knife before you bring it to the stone or strop block that you are using. If you don't, there are chances that you might contaminate the stone that you are working on more.

## Testing the Edge

There are many ways to test your edge to see if it is sharp enough. Everyone has their own favorite method, from seeing how well the blade cuts through the paper to carefully drawing the edge along a fingernail. In my opinion, the best way to test the edge is to use it. The efficiency at which it completes any given task helps to determine whether or not the edge was sharpened properly.

Another method to test out the edge (especially for our hunting knife) is to run the knife through a paper towel. If you can drag the knife through the towel without much resistance and by its own, then you have yourself a well-made and sharp knife.

# Bonus Chapter: Making Tongs

Now we are going to focus on making simple, but effective tongs that you can use in your metal works.

There are numerous materials that you can use for making your tongs. One of the more common materials that you can get your hands on is rebar. You can get one that is about 3 feet long and is about 1/2 thick.

- The first thing that you have to do is find the center of the bar. The make a mark on the bar using a permanent marker. From the center, measure 3 inches to the right and then 3 inches to the left. Call these two points A1 and A2.
- Now make an indent on A1 and A2. You can do this by placing the bar on the edge of your anvil and lightly tapping it. Using only the two indentations, you have a space of 6 inches in the center.
- Now take the rebar to your forge and heat the marked part.
- Bring over the bar back to the anvil and flatten the heated part. Strike on it using your hammer and make sure the entire 6 inches of the center is getting flatter. When they seem flat enough while still having about an inch or so of thickness, take the part back to the forge and heat it.
- Whenever you heat the bar, make sure that you are heating it to the yellow range temperature.
- Once the bar has been heated, bring it back to the anvil. Now we are going to use the horn part of the anvil (the little protrusion at the front). Place the heated part on the horn and then start striking the bar to bend it in such a manner, the two ends of the bar are going to meet. Strike the bar evenly so that when you create your tongs, you don't receive an uneven or awkward shape.
- Eventually, you are aiming to bring the two ends to a point where they look like they are making a 'U' shape. When you have achieved the shape, you have completed the first part of the process.
- Heat up one end of the bar and bring it to the yellow range temperature. Head over to the clamp and hold it firmly with the end pointing upwards. Now we are going to use a chisel and place it in the center of the base of the bar. Essentially, we are going to split the end. Line up the chisel in the center and strike it using a hammer. You can make the split as deep as possible but make sure that you do not overdo it.
- Repeat the above process on the other end of the bar as well. Basically heat it, clamp with the end pointing upwards and strike it so that you split it.
- The next step is going to involve the ends as well. This time, heat the ends and using the horn of the anvil, bend them inwards at a 90-degree angle.
- Start with one end of the bar and then work on the other end. In the end, you have both bars bending inwards. This formation becomes the hands of the tongs, holding any piece of material between them.

- Go back to the center of the bar. Heat it again and bring it back to the yellow temperature range. Remember those indentations that you had made? Choose a point slightly close to those indentations and strike the bar so that it starts bending inwards.
- Do the same with the other side of the bar as well.
- Now it looks like you have an indentation on both sides of the bar, close to where it bends to create the 'U' shape.
- When you have done that, you now have a very rudimentary form of tongs. You can use the bent ends to clamp down on any piece of metal and then bring it out of the forge easily.
- One tip for the process is to replace the rebar with coil springs because coil springs have that extra bit of elasticity to allow you to squeeze the two ends of the bar together.
- When you are using coil springs, make sure that you first start by cutting 3 feet of metal off the spring. Once done, you should then straighten the metal. Straightening a coil spring is relatively easy as the metal itself does not provide much resistance. Heat the parts that are bent and using a hammer, strike the metal lightly until it straightens.
- You can make use of many other metals for this, but rebar is easy to get while a coil spring makes for effective and flexible tongs.

# Conclusion

Bladesmithing is a satisfying process. The hard work that you put into it reaps some incredible results. Of course, it all depends on the efforts and the time you put into it.

Do not worry about the mistakes that you make. Every mistake is a learning curve for you. It is for this reason that the metals you are using in this book are easy to work with. Even if you do not get the right shape or perform a mistake during the grinding process, you don't have to worry about the metal. You can either choose to correct it easily or get yourself the metal (as it is fairly easy to get).

There really is something special about a razor-sharp knife that, once experienced, will be hard to live without. The superior cutting performance also factors in blade shape and geometry and ease of sharpening.

Always put yourself first. Are you in a safe environment? Are you keeping yourself protected? Are you staying a safe distance from fire and other harmful objects?

Remember, there is no point in trying something when you are not feeling safe.

Another factor that you must consider is that bladesmithing is a fairly time-consuming process. When you are aware of this, you might decide how best to approach the various processes. That is why, make sure that you are comfortable with one process before you carry on to the next. For example, if you feel like you are not doing the quenching right, then refer to this book and try again. Try not to skip to another step if you haven't properly performed the previous step.

You might find yourself physically exerting force on the metals you are working with. Sometimes, this might become a little uncomfortable. Rest your hands if you think that you are putting too much strain than is absolutely necessary. However, remember that if you follow the instructions in this book, then you won't have to strike the metal too hard.

Simply watching your blade come to life is one of the most enjoyable sensations you can experience. I am sincerely hoping that you have such an exquisite feeling yourself.

Keep yourself protected and enjoy a wonderful bladesmithing process.

And if you feel like it, drop a quick review for this book as well. I would really appreciate it.

Thanks again for tuning in to ForgeHero!

# References

Blandford, P. (2006). *Blacksmithing projects*. Mineola, N.Y.: Dover Publications.

Blandford, P. (2010). Practical blacksmithing and Metalworking. New York: TAB.

Parkinson, P. (2001). *The Artist Blacksmith*. Crowood Press.

Streeter, D. (2008). *Professional Smithing*. Lakeville, Minnesota: Astragal Press.

# Bladesmithing from Scrap Metal

## How to Make Knives with Leaf Springs, Cables, Railroad Spikes, and Files

# Introduction

I'm going to show you how you can forge blades using scrap metal, which you can probably find from a lot of different sources.

The one thing that you should pay attention to is the characteristics of scrap metal. Today, you can come into possession of high-quality carbon scrap steels and other alloys that the bladesmiths of long ago could have only dreamt of.

Notice the fact that I said 'carbon scrap steels'. You see, the main ingredient in steel is iron. However, the higher the carbon content, the better the metal will harden. If you find scrap made of stainless steel, then you may not be able to forge your blade readily. That is why, when looking for scrap, you should look for those that harden after processes such as heating or quenching.

But hardening is not the only thing you should be looking for when you are choosing your scrap. You should also pay attention to the type of steel that you are using. We will first start with some of the commonly used types of steel and which steel you should avoid.

Of course, we are going to delve into various scrap metals that you can use for forging as well, later on in the book.

On that note, welcome to the world of scrap bladesmithing!

# Chapter 1: Tests for Choosing the Right Scrap Steel

## Snap Test

When it comes to steel, you can check the carbon content of the material by using the snap test. You can also check the grain size.

In this test, take a small sample of the steel that you are planning to use and forge it to about 2-3mm thick. Ensure that it is about 3cm long and about 1cm wide. Once you have gotten the measurements right, heat the entire piece of metal to above non-magnetic levels. Then quench it in water to harden it to its full potential.

Next, take the metal and clamp it tightly using a tool like a vise. Take a hammer or a large tool that is capable of breaking the piece of metal (I recommend a hammer and in any case if you are working with metals it is important that you have a hammer around anyway!)

Strike the piece of metal with your hammer until it either bends to a 90-degree angle or breaks off completely.

Here's what the test results are if either of the above situations occur (bending or breaking):

- If the metal breaks without bending, then the metal has a high percentage of carbon.

- If it bends without breaking, then it has a relatively low percentage of carbon.

- If is bends partially and then breaks, then it is probably somewhere in the middle (an average percentage of carbon).

As mentioned above, it is not just the carbon level that you can check with this test. You can examine the steel and discover the grain size, too. The grain size gives you more information about the properties of the steel, such as the yield strength of the metal.

Usually, the smaller the grain size, the stronger the steel. This is because when the grain size is large, there is a greater chance for certain 'dislocations' or breakages to occur.

## Hardness Test

A snap test sounds convenient. But is there a test to gauge the hardness of the steel? Turns out, there is. Let's look at the Rockwell steel hardness test.

One of the characteristic features of the Rockwell test is that it is relatively easier to perform and has a higher degree of accuracy than other tests. You can also use this test on almost all forms of metal, which makes it useful for materials other than steel as well. The first thing that you need to do is find yourself a hard steel ball or a diamond tip that acts as an indenter.

You then need to perform a preliminary test. A certain amount of force is applied with the indenter to the piece of metal wherein it begins to break through the surface. The force leaves an indentation in the metal, which is then measured. This indentation is known as the baseline depth.

Next, an additional load is then added. This produces a deeper indentation, which is then measured as well. This particular indentation is known as the final depth. Once you have discovered both the baseline and final depth, you find the difference between the two values.

The resulting measurement is the hardness level of your metal.

But how can you find out if your steel is ready for you to forge it into a knife? Well, you use another simple, but effective, technique. All you have to do is heat the metal to its non-magnetic temperature. Once the metal reaches the temperature, you then quench it. If you discover that it hardens, then your metal is suitable for bladesmithing.

## The Risks With Scrap Metal

Finding scrap metal is easy and definitely works well for beginners and those who do not want to spend too much time obtaining the right materials.

But scrap metals come with its own challenges. Here are some:

1) These days, no two coil springs are the same. With the number of different vehicles on the roads, each vehicle manufacturer uses a unique set of coil springs. This means that different coil springs should be heat treated differently.

2) Another challenge you might find is that once you finish working on scrap metals, you might end up noticing hairline cracks. The presence of these cracks ruins the presentation of the entire tool.

3) Finally, the cracks can also reduce the durability of the metal and might even cause the metal to break entirely.

4) You are always going to have to expect the unexpected. When using scrap metal, you can never be certain of what you are working with.

5) Make sure that you know which steel you are using to make the knife. This will allow you to heat treat the knife properly.

# Chapter 2: Leaf Spring

Most leaf springs are made from 5160 steel. Refer to the properties section under Chapter 1 to find out more about 5160 steel.

## Normalizing

The next process that you are going to focus on is normalizing. It is good to normalize after you forge your knife because you can refine the grain of the steel. And refining the grain is important because it allows the hardness of the metal to increase.

1. For the normalizing process, heat up the knife to the yellow temperature range again; making sure that it is done slowly and uniformly.

2. Hold the knife at the temperature mentioned above for a period of time. You should ideally be normalizing your knife for one hour per one inch of thickness. This means that if your knife is two inches thick, then your normalizing period would be two hours.

3. After the normalizing duration, take out your knife and let it cool in the open air. Allow it to cool until it reaches room temperature.

4. Remember that normalizing is all about uniformity and you should ensure that the entire blade region of your knife is given a uniform normalizing treatment.

## Forging

Let's go with leaf springs to start things off.

1. You are initially going to get a lot of metal to work with. For this reason, you are going to use a hacksaw to cut off a small portion from both ends so that it makes it easier to work with the metal. Ideally, you can remove about one inch from each end.

2. The leaf springs you use will probably have a slight arc to them. You first have to take your hammer or any other heavy instrument and then hit the spring until it turns flat.

3. The best way to do this is not by striking the metal the just as it is. If you do that, you will probably end up hitting it a lot of times before you see any change at all.

4. Instead, first place the metal into the forge and heat it. Let it enter the yellow temperature range. The ideal forging temperature for leaf springs is in the yellow range.

5. Once that is done, place your piece of metal into an anvil and flatten it. Use your hammer for this. Strike the metal as much as possible until it is flattened. If you need to, you can place the metal back in the forge to heat it up again so that you hammer more easily.

6. Once the metal has been flattened, draw out the template of your knife on the spring.

7. Once that is done, use your hacksaw to cut out the shape of the knife.

8. Next, we are going to add the bevel. Take the knife over to the grinder and begin to slowly add the bevels. Take your time with this process so you can refine the shape of the knife.

9. After you have forged the knife, make sure that you have removed the scale. Once done, mark the holes that you would like to create into the handle of the knife and then use a drill to make the actual holes.

10. Grind out any bevels in the knife and give it a smooth finish.

## Annealing

1. Once again, you are going to heat the knife to its transformation range (the yellow range). At this point, you can check to see if the knife is magnetic or not. Simply take your magnet and bring it close to the metal.

2. If the metal is still magnetic, then heat it a bit more and check again. When the knife is truly non-magnetic, then take it out of the forge and get ready for the quenching process.

## Quenching

Most people think that they have to invest a lot into the quenching process. But the reality is that you actually don't have to.

You can get yourself food-grade quenching oils. They are a lot cheaper than commercial quenching oils. They are also easily available. You just need to drop by your local store to find them.

Two of the most common oils used for quenching are canola and peanut oil. The main reason for choosing these two oils is the high flash point that they have, which is ideal for the quenching process. Before you quench the metal into the oil, make sure that you preheat them anywhere between 120-130 degrees Fahrenheit. Quench the knife for about 11 seconds.

## Tempering

You temper the steel immediately after hardening. When the knife cools down, you reheat it to a temperature between 302-752°F.

For the leaf spring, you can use a regular oven for the tempering process. All you have to do is preheat the oven to 375°F. Let the oven preheat completely before you place the steel inside. Once the metal is inside, keep it there for about three hours at that temperature. You can place your metal directly on the oven rack or you can put it on top of a baking sheet.

Don't have an oven? Then you can use a toaster if your metal can fit inside. Or alternatively, you can use the toaster if you are planning to prepare some cookies in the oven!

If you have neither of the equipment above or if they are both engaged, then the best way to temper the steel is by using a blowtorch. You need to focus the flame from the blowtorch on the area that you want hardened. You will know when the tempering process is complete when the blade turns a blue color.

Finally, you are ready to grind the bevels and fix the handle. Once you have attached it, sharpen the knife until you give it the edge that you want. To finish off the process, polish the knife and the handle to add that extra special gleam to it.

Your knife is now ready.

# Chapter 3: Cable Damascus Knife

Working with a cable is not difficult. You might think it is a complicated process, but what you really need to understand is that you have to be patient with it.

The first thing to remember is that you should not pick stainless wire for your knife. This is because when you are working with the welding process, you might find out that stainless wire does not get welded into the billet. Additionally, it is also toxic to work with stainless wire.

Here is the process you need to follow for a cable (Damascus knife):

1. Start off by either arc-welding the cable or tying up the end of the cable. This will prevent the cable from unlaying, wherein the strands of the cable begin to come off.

2. Place the cable into tar or oil; making sure that it is soaked completely.

3. Take it out of the tar or oil and then place it into the forge. There is often a debate about when the metal is ready after placing it into the forge. You should let the tar or oil burn out completely.

4. Once you have noticed the tar and oil burn out, use your tongs and flux the metal. Ideally, you should be using borax for this process. Make sure you flux the metal liberally, with particular focus on the center. Try and get the flux to soak into the metal. The main purpose of the flux is to prevent oxidization. You also ensure the metal is fluid and remove any other form of impurities.

5. Next, heat the metal again. Take it out of the fire, brush the metal, and then flux it again. Take it back into the forge and heat it again.

6. At this point, you are ready to hammer the cable. Take out your hammer and pound on the cable lightly. Once done, place it back into the forge and bring the color of the cable to roughly the same color as inside the forge. When you feel like the color has been attained, take it out of the forge and get ready to weld it.

7. To weld, make sure that the ends of the cable are brought together. Weld it until it has a nice rectangular shape. There are two ways of welding the ends together:

   a. You can take the cable to its welding temperature. Then transfer it to a vise and twist the ends together.

   b. Or, you can simply use the hammer for the ends.

8. It is time to forge the cable. When you are forging, remember that when you first bring the hammer to the cable, your blows should be soft and precise. Do not strike it too hard or you might risk damages on the cable. While you are hammering, roll the cable around and make sure that your blows strike the cable evenly from one end to the other.

9. Once you are done hammering, run it through the flux process again. Use a wire brush on the cable's surface, making sure you brush it all over. You only need to run the brush a couple of times on the cable.

10. Next, grind out the bevels.

11. Now you are going to heat-treat the blade. We start with the normalizing process. We are going to use a kaowool on the blade, which is essentially a type of insulator. Cover the tip of the blade with a kaowool and place the knife into the forge. This way, you ensure that the entire blade receives the heat treatment evenly. Heat up the metal to around 1,300°F and then place the metal inside the forge for an hour. Come back and allow the metal to cool in air for an hour. Repeat this once more.

12. Once you have finished the normalizing process, make sure that you remove the kaowool so that you can get it ready for the quenching process.

13. Once you have removed the kaowool, dip the blade into the quenching liquid of your choice.

14. Your heat treatment is done and you are ready to attach the handle.

15. Fix the handle.

16. Sharpen the knife.

17. Polish the blade and handle.

# Chapter 4: Railroad Spike

When you are getting started with forging or if you are still getting used to the process, one of the ways that you can forge is by using a railroad spike. This is ideal for those who are just entering the world of bladesmithing or those who are simply out of touch with the various techniques.

One of the common misconceptions about railroad spikes is that they are a material with high carbon content. It is true that bladesmiths around the world have used railroad spikes to craft a blade, but they do not have the carbon content that most think they do. The reason that bladesmiths enjoy using them is that they are almost readily available and usually for free.

The misunderstanding about their high carbon content comes from the fact that there are some railroads marked with the letters 'HC' for 'High Carbon.' But what that means is that though there is a high carbon content for the manufacturing of railroads, it is not high enough for blade making.

What is high carbon for railroads is low carbon for knifemakers.

Here is something to remember:

Based on specifications set forth by American Railway Engineering Association, railroad spikes can be divided into two categories: low carbon track spikes that are used on those sections of railroads that are straight, and high carbon steel track spikes used on switches and curves. The association's guidelines mention that, low carbon spikes may contain no more than 0.12% carbon and "High Carbon" spikes may contain no more than 0.30% carbon.

But how does this affect knife makers? Well, to make a good knife, the blade needs to contain anywhere between 0.85% to 1.5% carbon.

That is three times or more than the carbon content contained in railroad spikes.

But why use such low amounts of carbon in railroad spikes? Aren't they supposed to be harder in order to keep the rail tracks together? The reasoning behind the low carbon is that the spikes can bend a little. A bent spike can hold the rail track but a broken one (due to high carbon) will not be able to hold the track together for a long time.

Thus, this is why you cannot use a railroad spike for making tools that you will use regularly, such as knives. Railroad spikes do not have a high enough carbon content and they easily suffer cracks on the surface.

However, it is easy to start with railroad spikes and get yourself acclimated to the various processes involved in forging.

That said, if you have received an order from a customer to make a knife, then you should not be using railroad spikes for it.

1. When working with railroad spikes, it is important to note that many of them do not survive the hammering process if they are heated to temperatures below 1,200°F. What do I mean by the fact that they don't survive? Well, they are easily prone to breakage and cracking. For this reason, you should start the process by heating the spike to temperatures between 1,200°F to 1,500°F.

2. Here's something you *can* do with the railroad spike. Once you have heated the spike to the temperature mentioned above, you can add designs to it if you wish. You can do this by placing the spike between a vise and twisting it. When you are twisting, make sure that you only focus on doing half rotations or full ones so that you can keep the point of the spike pointing in one direction.

3. Heat up the spike again. This time forge it into the shape of the knife that you would like to attain. The longer you want the tip to be, the more times you might have to put the knife in the forge to attain the desired effect.

4. It's time for the grind. When you reach this process, you are going to ensure that you clean off the scale and grind away whatever you do not want on the knife. Take your time with this step so that you have results that you are satisfied with. You should also make sure that you grind a bevel and an edge.

5. Your knife is looking good and you are almost ready to finish the process. Some people decide to polish the blade at this point, but it is highly recommended that you do not do so. If you are punching holes, make sure that you do it now before the heat treatment process. We are going to heat treat the blade at this point so let's get into that process.

6. First, gradually heat the spike in the forge until it reaches the orange range. You can check and see if it has reached the non-magnetic stage at this point. If it hasn't, then heat the spike a little more until it reaches the non-magnetic point.

7. Once that is done, take the spike out of the forge and quench it in the liquid of your choice.

8. Now we are going to use a method to see how smooth your knife has turned out. Use a file and run it against the knife. If the file slides along your knife, then you have worked through the hardening process wonderfully.

9. Once you have quenched the spike, lift it out of the liquid and temper it. As we had noticed in Chapter 2, you can temper it in the oven by preheating the oven to anywhere between 350-400°F. You can also use your toaster if the knife can fit into it. Or you can make use of the blowtorch as mentioned above. The choice is entirely yours.

10. Now, you can add the handle on the knife. When you are going to move the knife to the scales, make sure you wipe off the inside of the scales before you apply epoxy. This ensures the scales will be dry.

11. Right before the final step, make sure that you use acetone to clean up the knife. You can then apply a coat of varnish.

12. For the final step, you just have to polish and run the knife through one more stage of sharpening.

13. With that, you have completed working on the knife.

# Chapter 5: Coil Spring

A coil spring is an important component of any vehicle. It is an elastic component (though not *that* elastic), which helps the vehicle absorb shocks. It usually takes in the shock and gently puts it back in the direction of the ground in such a manner that it prevents any damage to the vehicle itself.

But when they are not used in vehicles, they can be used to make some rather decent knives. It is true, however, that you might have to make thinner knives when you are using them.

Forging a knife from coil spring can be a bit of a challenge. But despite the challenge, coil springs are still an ideal steel for making knives. One of the more difficult parts of working with a coil spring is trying to straighten it. People often try numerous ways and give up in exasperation.

But luckily, there is a good technique to easily straighten out the coil without tearing out your hair in frustration. It has to do with the anvil. But first, let us check and see if the coil is ideal for forging.

This is an important step, because sometimes you may eventually find small hairline cracks that you would not have seen earlier. So go ahead and examine your metal carefully to check for those. You should ideally aim to get a coil spring that does not have many of the aforementioned cracks. Coil springs of older vehicles are preferred because they have 5160 steel in them, which is ideal for knifemaking. To understand how old the vehicle has to be, check and see if it was manufactured 10 years before. If so, then you have yourself some nice steel to work with.

One of the important things to remember is that you need to plan out the knife that you are going to make when you get your hands on the coil spring. You may not have enough metal to make a broad blade. Instead think about something narrow, so that you can forge accordingly.

Your first step is to use a small part of the coil and heat it. Ideally, choose an end of the coil for this purpose and if your coil is ready for forging, you can use the other end to work on your knife.

1. Heat the coil until it reaches the orange range. Then quench the coil in the liquid of your choice. Check and see if the coil hardens. If it does, then you can use it for knifemaking. If it doesn't, you will unfortunately have to find another coil.

2. To straighten out the coil spring, make sure that you cut it off short. Once that is done, you can use the hardy hole that comes with the anvil to hold the spring in place while you straighten it. First, take the entire coil and cut off a half portion of it using an electric saw in such a way that it resembles the shape of a horseshoe. Next, place the cut out coil into the forge and heat it until it enters the orange range. Place the hot coil into the hardy hole of the anvil and bend it using your tongs until it straightens. And that's all there is to it!

3. Once it is straightened, you can then use your hammer to flatten it more. At this point, you should be looking to flatten it in such a way that you start noticing the shape of your

knife. You might need multiple turns at the forge to get the right shape, but eventually, you will be able to make it work.

4. After flattening out the coil and straightening it into the shape that you want, you can then cut off any additional length from the metal. A simple saw will do the trick (since at this point it is not too thick to provide too much resistance).

5. In your hands, you now have the crude shape of your knife. We are going to work on it until we get it to the finished product that we desire.

6. Now it is time for the forging process. Place the knife into the forge and wait until heats up to the orange range. Take out the knife and then use your hammer to make the knife shape.

7. Take your knife to the grind next and add the bevel to it. Smoothen out the surface and remove any markings or remnants of the coil springs from it.

8. Take out your trust drill. We are going to drill holes into the handle. Punch in the desired number of holes into the handle based on the design you are going for. When you have finished adding the holes, your knife will actually look like it's finished. But the real work is far from over. We are now going to send it to the forge.

9. If you would like to see whether the steel is okay and if there is anything wrong or amiss about it, try and etch it using ferric chloride. One of the important uses of the ferric chloride is to remove any phosphorus and to reduce hydrogen sulfide. Essentially, you are making sure that the quality of the steel that you are working with is up to your preferred.

10. Once you have ascertained the quality of the steel, place it into the forge and allow it to heat until it reaches the orange range. At this point, we are only focusing on heat treatment. So as soon as your metal has reached the required temperature, shift it immediately into a quenching liquid.

11. You need to be sure get the right temperature for this process. Place the knife into the forge until it reaches around 1,500°F. Once the temperature has been reached, take out the knife and dip it into a quenching liquid. For this metal, ideally I would recommend that you use canola oil. Make sure that you preheat the canola up to a temperature of 400°F.

12. You need to heat treat the metal for two 2-hour cycles. Essentially, you are going to follow the above steps and ensure that the knife receives a heat treatment for the full two hours. Once done, you have to repeat the process again, making sure it once again receives the heat treatment for two hours.

13. With that, you have completed the heat treatment for the blade.

14. Once again, take the knife to a grinder and make sure that you remove the scaling from the heat treatment. Use the grinder or sharpening stone to bring the edge of the knife to

your desired state. Smoothen out the surface if necessary.

15. With that, you are done with the coil spring knife. The final step basically involves merely adding the handle to the knife.

# Chapter 6: Knife From a Nicholson File

When you are using a file, you should keep in mind a few important things when getting started. The first is that you should ideally aim to work with a file that has at least 0.9% carbon. Along with the carbon content however, you need look for additional mixes. You should have a little manganese and trace amounts of chromium, vanadium, and tungsten. With these combinations, you are going to get a metal that has a good level of hardness. Luckily, with a Nicholson file, you are getting a truly hard steel.

Why is it such hard steel? That is because a file is mainly created in order to cut through metal.

Nicholson files have a sense of consistency. This means that no matter what Nicholson file you use, they are always made of the same metal: **1095.**

In order to make a knife using a file, you must make sure that you soften the file before you proceed with the knifemaking (since it is hardened to be used as a file). However, you can still make a knife without the softening process. Which brings us to the following two options:

- The first option is that you can directly use the hard file to make your knife. The result will be rather crude and it might look aesthetically unpleasing. But it is the fastest and simplest method to make your knife. You could try this method if you would like to practice a bit, but there are also other ways you can practice making a knife, as we had seen earlier chapters.

- The second option is to subject the file to the softening process, which in this case is annealing. With this process, you can soften the metal and create a knife that not only looks visually pleasing, but also looks more like a knife than a prison shank (which might be the case if you are using the first method). Obviously, you get a better knife using this process, so let's go ahead and expand on option number two.

We have to start off with the annealing process.

1. Use your forge and heat the blade to a temperature of 1,350°F. We are going to use the magnet trick to check and see how hot the metal really is. If the magnet sticks to the surface, continue heating it until you have reached the non-magnetic temperature. If you like, you can also use a torch to heat the surface of the file evenly.

2. Eventually, you will notice that the magnet stops being attracted to the metal. At this point, you might notice that the color of the metal is red hot. Keep the metal at the red-hot range for about 2-3 minutes (after making sure the metal is non-magnetic).

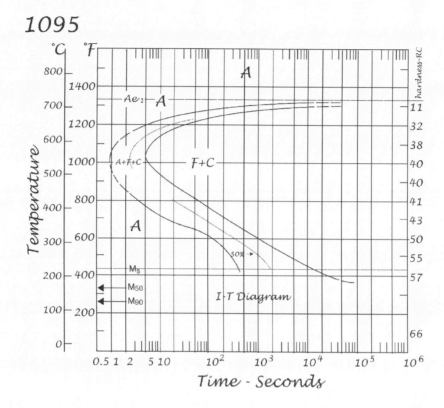

3. Allow the blade to cool off in the air. You should be able to watch as the glow begins to reduce. When it reaches a dull red glow, quench the blade. You can use Vermiculite. Wood ash is another option for you to choose from. Make sure that whatever option you choose, it covers at least six inches all the way around. The more it covers, the better your knife will turn out to be.

4. Once you have quenched it, the blade will be left in a softened state.

5. Your steel has now been properly annealed is ready to be treated all processes required to turn it into a knife.

6. Take out your trusted drill and make the holes into the tang. Use as many holes as required, based on your preferences.

7. Head over to the grinder and shape the profile of the knife. Whenever you notice the file getting hot, stop your work and dip the knife into water to cool it. You should keep the temperature of the file under 450°F. This might be difficult to manage but the trick is to cool the knife immediately whenever you notice that it is getting too hot. Do not wait to see how much heat you can handle. If you are not sure when to dip it into the water, just go ahead and cool the metal even if it gets just a little hot.

8. Another way to notice if the knife is getting too hot is to look for blue spots. When you notice these spots, it means you are heating up the knife too much. Try to avoid reaching this point, but use them as emergency limiters to ensure that you do not ruin the knife any further. If you end up having too many blue spots, the knife might become too soft in the final grinding process. Hence, the importance of giving extra attention to this during the process to avoid any complications in the future.

9. When you have created a profile of the knife, begin grinding the bevels. Eventually, your knife will look more like the shape you want. When you reach this point, smoothen out the knife and refine the shape as much as you can. (The guide to doing a flat grind on your blade is at the end of this book)

10. Harden the steel to just above its non-magnetic temperature.

11. For the next step, you are going to temper the steel. To do this, we can use the kitchen oven. Simply preheat the oven to a temperature of 450°F. Place the metal into the oven and allow it to heat up. Let the metal remain in the oven for about two hours.

12. Take out the metal and allow it to cool down to room temperature. When it is cool, take it back into the oven and let it heat for another two hours. This time, when the two-hour cycle is complete, you are going to cool it down with water.

13. We are going to use sandpaper to remove any marks from the knife. Take out some 100-grit sandpaper for this process and begin sanding the knife. Sand both sides of the knife and work your way to all the surfaces, including the handle. You are going to get a well-shaped and smooth knife from this. You will notice that the edge is not sharp yet, but that is alright. We will come back to sharpening it later.

14. Now, switch to a 220-grit sandpaper and repeat the process. Make sure that you start with both sides of the knife. Finally, use the 400-grit sandpaper. Your knife will start giving out a nice shine.

15. With that, your blade is ready to receive a handle. If you have already prepared your handle, you can attach it to the knife at this point.

16. At this point, you can begin to sharpen the blade. Take out a sharpening stone and work on the edge of the knife until you can see it reach your preferred sharpness.

# Chapter 7: Scrap Damascus

In this method, you will be trying to take different pieces of metals and then piling them one on top of the other.

For this purpose, you are better off working with bandsaw blades and files.

Let's look at each of the materials that you are going to use. When using bandsaw blades, remember that you might come across different saws that have different qualities. You should first be looking at the band saw blade diameter. This tells you which bandsaw you can use for which blade and more importantly, which bandsaw can be used to cut the blade.

If you choose to make blades that are thicker, then they can withstand more strain from straight cuts. On the other hand, when you are using thinner blades, they are perfect for some of the lighter work that you do. But the best way to choose the right bandsaw is by trying to figure out the width of the knife that you are creating.

With this in mind, you can use the handy table below to get an idea of which bandsaw is perfect for your blade width.

| Wheel Diameter (inches) | Blade Thickness (inches) |
| --- | --- |
| 4 – 6 | .014 |
| 6 – 8 | .018 |
| 8 – 10 | .020 |
| 11 – 18 | .025 |
| 18 – 24 | .032 |
| 24 – 30 | .035 |
| 30+ | .042, .050, .063 |

Using the chart above, you can find out the ideal bandsaw for the right blade.

1. The next part is cutting the bandsaw and the file so that you can allow them to be stacked on top of each other. We are going to be using a bandsaw to cut the bandsaw that you have in your hands. Refer to the table above to choose the right bandsaw for cutting the file and the bandsaw.

2. Make sure that you cut all the pieces to have the same dimensions.

3. Next, take out the grinding wheel and then smoothen out the surfaces of the files and the

bandsaws. Remove as much of the marks as possible so that there are no chances of cracks forming on the surface during the forging process.

4. Once you have done that, you need to get the plates to 'stick' together. It is only then that you will be able to drop the metal pieces into the forge and then continue with your project. To make them stick, you need to weld the pieces of metal together.

5. Start by welding the corners of the metal. This will allow you to put them together without them easily falling apart, especially when you add them to the forge.

6. Once the welding process has been completed, you are then ready to use the forge. Place the piece of metal you are holding into the forge. Wait for it to heat up. As the metal continues to heat, take it out using the tongs and flux it with borax. Alternate between heating and adding flux until you notice the metal reach the yellow range.

7. When the metal is glowing yellow, you can take it out of the forge and then gently use the hammer to set the weld in. What this means is that you are hammer the metal so that all the pieces begin to like one large block of metal rather than smaller pieces of metal.

8. Once you have completed this process, you will notice that the original weld that you had placed on the metal is still there. It will look like small mounds on the corners of your metal. The best way to get rid of these mounds is by using a saw. Make sure that you are especially careful while trying to cut the welds or you might accidentally cut of a piece of metal or maybe even add a little dent in it.

9. When you have finally removed the welds, you need to place it back into the forge. Allow it to enter the yellow range of heat and take out the metal. Hammer it until you do not notice any visible signs of the welding process or any indication that there are different metals stuck together.

10. Next, head over to the grinder and take out any unevenness or marks that are on the metal. Continue with the grind until you have a nice even shape in front of you. At this point, your piece of metal should look like a rectangular block of solid steel without any indications of indentations, lines, or cracks.

11. If you want to create your knife from this metal, you only have to follow the steps below. You are basically going to go through the typical forging process.

12. Head over to your forge and place the steel into it. Wait until it turns hot enough that it enters the yellow range. Once it is in the range, you can take it out and begin hammering it. Get the shape of your knife into the metal. You might have a rudimentary design of your knife at this point, but that it just fine. We are going to be adding in more details once we are done with this step.

13. Head over to the grinder and begin getting your shape fine-tuned. Once you have done that, you can then subject it to the heat treatment process.

# Chapter 8: Anvil From a Railroad Track

One of the best parts about working with an anvil is the fact that you actually only need a few simple tools to complete the process. This might be contrary to what most people believe. In fact, one of the common misconceptions about making an anvil is that people think they are going to have to invest in a lot of equipment to work on the railroad track in order to finally change it into the shape that they desire. In reality, you are not going to be involved in such a complicated process, as we will notice below.

When you are working with railroad tracks you have to make sure that you are choosing the right one.

There are a few different types. First, you have a railroad track that is made for large trains and locomotives. And then you have the tracks that are made for smaller carriages. What kind of smaller carriages? Well think of those wagons that are used in mines.

Since you are making an anvil, you need to have a railroad track that is on the bigger end of things. Which is why you should be looking for used railroad tracks from trains.

When you are looking for tracks that you would like to work with, you should go for the 100-pounds/yard tracks. As for the length of the rail, you should go for one that is a foot long.

When you have the track with you, you should focus on creating a hardy hole (which we saw earlier as being used to straighten a piece of metal). You might start off with a small hole and once you have made it, you are going to expand it even more. In order to achieve that expansion, you are going to make use of a large punch or chisel for the job. Below is a diagram of what we will try to achieve with the railroad track.

1. Take out your chisel and using the hammer, punch through the hole until you see it getting bigger.

2. Now you have a foot-long railroad track with you. But it doesn't actually look anything like an anvil now, does it? For that reason, we are going to trace the shape of the anvil on top of the railroad track.

3. Take out a chalk and face the anvil lengthwise. You are now facing the width of the anvil. Find the midpoint along the width. We will call this point 'Point A.' Essentially, you need to focus on one end of the railroad track, find the midpoint, and mark it. Once done, draw a line that connects the midpoints of one end of the railroad track to the other end of the railroad track.

4. Once you have drawn the line, you now need to find the midpoint on that line. Once done, draw the second line across the midpoint of the first line, such that they connect the two sides of the anvil. You can name the point on one side as 'Side A' and the one of the other side as 'Side B.' Basically, you now have a cross shape on the top face of the railroad track and you have further split the top face into four equal sections.

5. Now comes the tricky part. Start from Point A and trace a curved line to Side A. You can choose to draw a straight line; but in order to get the right shape of an anvil, I prefer a

curved line. Next, draw another curved line from Point A and connect it to Side B.

6.  You now probably have a rough triangle shape on one end of the top of your anvil. The next step is fairly easy. All you have to do is take out your electric saw and then cut along the specific lines. Here are the lines you should focus on:

    a.  Cut along the line that connects Point A to Side A.

    b.  Cut along the line that connects Point A to Side B.

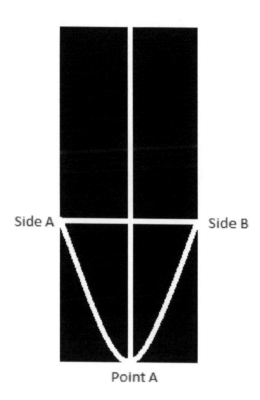

The image above represents the top view of the railroad track that you have chosen. It might or might not be a perfect rectangle, but the above design is what you should ideally aim for when making your anvil.

7.  With the cuts done, it is time to subject the anvil to the grinder. You are going to smoothen the surface and give your anvil the finish that it requires.

8.  If you like, you can also make use of a polish to give your anvil a nice shine.

9.  With this, you have completed your anvil.

# Chapter 9: Understanding Different Steels & Processes

When you are choosing a blade for forging, there are different factors that you must consider. What exactly are you going to use the blade for? Will you be using it only for cutting or also for utility purposes? Will it hold an edge for a long time? Do you want it to be flexible?

Here are some of the common metals that are used by bladesmiths:

O-1

## Content

| Element | Percentage of Element in Steel |
|---------|-------------------------------|
| Carbon | 0.90% |
| Chrome | 0.50% |
| Manganese | 1.00% |
| Tungsten | 0.50% |

## Properties

| Properties | Details |
|------------|---------|
| Wear Resistance | Medium |
| Toughness | Medium |
| Red Hardness | Low |
| Distortion in Heat Treating | Very Low |
| Forging | Start at 1,800 to 1,950°F |
| Quench | Oil |
| Tempering | 350 to 500°F |

0-1 is a pretty standard carbon steel for forging almost all kinds of blades, except the larger ones (such as swords). It has been known to be quite forgiving when subjected to warping or heat treatment. This makes the metal easy to work with during the heat treatment process.

## W-1

### Content

| Element | Percentage of Element in Steel |
|---|---|
| Carbon | 0.60 - 1.4% |

| Properties | Details |
|---|---|
| Wear Resistance | Medium |
| Toughness | Medium |
| Red Hardness | Very Low |
| Forging | Anywhere from 1,800 to 1,900°F |
| Hardening | Anywhere from 1,400 to 1,550°F |
| Quench | Water or Oil |
| Tempering | Anywhere from 350 to 650°F |

This steel is a general-purpose steel where you can get a uniform depth because of its high level of hardness.

## WHC

### Properties

| Element | Percentage of Element in Steel |
|---|---|
| Carbon | 0.75% |

| Properties | Details |
|---|---|
| Wear Resistance | Medium |

| | |
|---|---|
| Toughness | High Medium |
| Red Hardness | Very Low |
| Forging | Anywhere from 1,850 to 1,900°F |
| Hardening | Anywhere from 1,400 to 1,550°F |
| Quench | Water or Oil |
| Tempering | Anywhere from 350 to 650°F |

WHC has a slightly lower carbon content that W-1. However, what it lacks in the carbon department, it makes up for in the shock resistance department, with its ability to withstand shocks better than W-1.

## 10-Series Steels

## Properties of 1050

| Element | Percentage of Element in Steel |
|---|---|
| Carbon | 0.48 - 0.55% |
| Manganese | 0.60 - 0.90% |

## Properties of 1060

| Element | Percentage of Element in Steel |
|---|---|
| Carbon | 0.55 - 0.65% |
| Manganese | 0.60 - 0.90% |

## Properties of 1070

| Element | Percentage of Element in Steel |
|---|---|
| Carbon | 0.65 - 0.75% |
| Manganese | 0.60 - 0.90% |

## Properties of 1080

| Element | Percentage of Element in Steel |
| --- | --- |
| Carbon | 0.75 - 0.88% |
| Manganese | 0.60 - 0.90% |

## Properties of 1095

| Element | Percentage of Element in Steel |
| --- | --- |
| Carbon | 0.90 - 1.03% |
| Manganese | 0.30 - 0.50% |

## Common Properties Shared by the Metals in 10-series

| Properties | Details |
| --- | --- |
| Wear Resistance | Medium |
| Toughness | High to Medium, based on the carbon content |
| Red Hardness | Very Low |
| Forging | Anywhere from 1,750 to 1,850°F |
| Hardening | Anywhere from 1,400 to 1,550°F |
| Quench | Oil |
| Tempering | Anywhere from 300 to 500°F |

When people think about which are the usable alloys for bladesmithing they are referring to the 10-series. What makes them ideal for making blades is that they are pretty stable and you can shape them easily under the hammer as compared to many other forms of steel.

# 5160

## Properties

| Element | Percentage of Element in Steel |
|---|---|
| Carbon | 0.56 - 0.64% |
| Chromium | 0.70 - 0.90% |
| Manganese | 0.75 - 1.00% |
| Phosphorus | Maximum of 0.035% |
| Silicon | 0.15 - 0.35% |
| Sulphur | Maximum of 0.04% |

| Properties | Details |
|---|---|
| Wear Resistance | High |
| Toughness | High |
| Red hardness | Low |
| Forging | Beginning from 1,800°F |
| Hardening | Anywhere from 1,450 |

Also popularly known as 'spring steel,' 5160 has high durability and excellent toughness. It is a medium carbon steel well suited for axes, swords, and other large blades.

# L-6

## Properties

| Element | Percentage of Element in Steel |
|---|---|
| Carbon | 0.70 - 0.90% |
| Chromium | 0.03% |
| Manganese | 0.35 - 0.55% |

| | |
|---|---|
| Nickel | 1.4 - 2.6% |
| Phosphorus | 0.025% |
| Silicon | 0.25% |
| Vanadium | 0.15% |

| Properties | Details |
|---|---|
| Wear Resistance | Medium |
| Toughness | Very High |
| Red Hardness | Low |
| Forging | Anywhere from 1,800 to 2,000°F |
| Quench | Oil |
| Hardening | Anywhere from 1,450 to 1,550°F |
| Tempering | Anywhere from 300 to 500°F |

This steel is ideal if you are working with large saw blades and other similar items with broad blades.

## S-1

## Properties

| Element | Percentage of Element in Steel |
|---|---|
| Carbon | 0.50% |
| Chromium | 1.50% |
| Tungsten | 2.50% |

| Properties | Details |
|---|---|
| Wear Resistance | Medium |

| | |
|---|---|
| Toughness | High |
| Red Hardness | Medium |
| Forging | Anywhere from 1,850 to 2,050°F |
| Hardening | Anywhere from 1,650 to 1,750°F |
| Quench | Oil |
| Tempering | 400 to 450°F |

This steel is designed to resist long-term effects of wear and abrasion. In fact, it has been formed to absorb shocks. Its main purpose is making pneumatic and hand tools for riveting and chipping.

## S-5

## Properties

| Element | Percentage of Element in Steel |
|---|---|
| Carbon | 0.55% |
| Manganese | 80% |
| Molybdenum | 0.40% |
| Silicon | 2% |

| Properties | Details |
|---|---|
| Wear Resistance | Medium |
| Toughness | Very High |
| Red Hardness | Medium |
| Forging | Anywhere from 1,650 to 1,800°F |
| Hardening | Anywhere from 1,600 to 1,700°F |
| Quench | Oil |
| Tempering | 350 to 450°F |

You use the S-5 for the same tools as the S-1. However, the S-5 is much tougher because of the molybdenum content.

Let us now look at the different processes:

## Normalizing

The process of forging is very stressful on steel. The repeated cycles of heating and cooling, along with the physical rearrangement of the metal, creates havoc on the grain structure. Large or irregular grains can create weaknesses in your blade. This can lead to shattering or breaking during the process of making your knife or later on while the blade is being used. By normalizing your steel, you can press the reset button on your steel's grain and ensure this doesn't happen.

In fact, one of the most important parts of this is the fact that you can use it if you have made any mistakes that you would like to rectify.

In this process, you heat the metal to a particularly high temperature and then take it out to air cool. The metal gradually returns to room temperature.

## Annealing

Some people wonder whether annealing is even necessary in the forging of blades. It is.

There are two main reasons for annealing:

- The first is to soften it and remove stress on the blade.

- The second is to make the structure of the blade even.

Every time a piece of metal is worked it accumulates stress and gets harder. The harder it gets, the more difficult it is to work again. But how exactly is annealing done?

The entire process is simple.

The metal is heated up, held at temperature for a time, and then it is slow cooled. Usually, when someone says that the metal has to be slow cooled, they are referring to the fact that it is left to cool inside the forge itself, allowing the metal to slowly return to room temperature.

Wait a minute!

Doesn't the annealing process sound suspiciously similar to the normalizing process? Can't we just call them annealing and well, annealing again?

Though it might be tempting, there is a difference.

You see, in annealing, you leave the metal in the forge. This means that it takes longer for the metal to cool down. In the normalizing process however, you are subjecting the metal to air at room temperature.

Does it make a difference?

Absolutely it does!

The main reason we anneal a metal (or in other words, allow it to cool slowly) is because of the following reasons:

- You increase the strength of the metal. You really don't want your knife breaking when all you did was use it to cut some zucchini! Annealing adds that extra durability to your knife.

- It improves the metal's ductility. A metal's ductility decides how much it can stretch before it breaks. Most knives have the capacity to bend a little to absorb shock. If they were always rigid, then they would wear easily. The best way to understand this is by using the example of our legs. When you jump from a certain elevated platform and land on the ground, you bend your knees slightly to absorb the shock and distribute it evenly throughout your body. If you do not bend, then the shock becomes focused on one region, leading to injuries. The same concept applies to knives as well. If they can bend slightly, then they have the ability to absorb more shocks. But don't worry, it does not mean that your knife is going to behave like a limp piece of cloth.

- You can easily elongate the knife without worrying about degrading the quality. Sometimes, when you want to make the blade a little bit longer, you might end up creating cracks on the surface. To avoid such scenarios, we subject the metal to the annealing process.

## Quenching

This is a pretty popular process in metallurgy and you might have seen it being performed on TV or in the movies. Basically, the metal worker takes the steel and then dips it into a cauldron, often creating a dramatic effect. You can see steam rising and the water sizzling as the metal cools. However, water is not the only medium that the metal worker uses for the process of quenching. Before we dive into that, let us look at the quenching process in more detail.

Quenching is a process that occurs after another process where the metal is heated to high temperatures. Examples of such processes preceding quenching are annealing (which we looked at earlier) or normalizing (which we shall look at in the next section). In both annealing and normalizing, the cooling process can take some time. This could affect the strength of the steel, causing it to lower more than necessary. Through quenching, you are lowering the temperature considerably, which could benefit the work that you are doing. Metal workers usually apply this method so that they can prevent the cooling process from altering the molecular structure of the metal.

Quenching is typically done by submerging the metal immediately to a certain liquid, typically water, or forced air. In a forced air-cooling system, the air is pushed out through specially arranged ducts that help in, you guessed it, cooling the temperature of an object quickly. The water or air used for the process of quenching is termed the 'medium.'

Now you might think to yourself: Is there any other liquid that can be used for quenching? That is actually a valid point. We are so used to seeing the movies show metallic objects such as swords and weapons being dipped into water that we are not aware of any other liquids that can be used. However, here a couple of other liquids that are used for quenching:

## Oil

There are numerous oil options that you can use for the process of quenching. You have fish oils, vegetable oils, and certain mineral oils that can help you attain the desired effect. With each medium, you have a different rate of cooling. When you use oil, you are using a liquid that has a higher cooling rate than air but cools the metal down more slowly than water.

When choosing oils, here are a few options that you can consider for your bladesmithing requirements:

Food Grade Oils

Many bladesmiths and knifemakers utilize food grade oils for the sole reason that they are cheaper and readily available. You can head over to your local supermarket or store and find some on their shelves. In fact, you are also spoilt for choice, with the number of different brands available to you. One famous food oil used in quenching is canola oil.

During the quenching and tempering processes, food oils spread a much more bearable odor than other types of oil. While you might think that this is a minor point to make note of, it might affect you if you have a workshop attached to your home or within your home.

To quench in food grade oils, preheat the oil to anywhere between 150°F and 200°F.

Motor Oil

Another oil that is popularly used in the knifemaking industry or among knifemaking hobbyists is motor oil. People use both new and used motor oil, depending on their requirements. The advantage of motor oil is that it is really cheap to obtain. In fact, used motor oil is free; you may have it in your garage, you might find some in your friend's garage, or even in the local store.

However, do note that used motor oil tends to leave a stench. Additionally, you might find a dark film coating the blade you are working on, which is quite difficult to remove. Another reason why you might want to stay away from used motor oil is the fact that it contains quite a few toxins that could be potentially harmful if inhaled. For beginners, it is highly recommended that they do not use motor oils. Experienced knife makers who have worked with the blade for many years might be able to spot good motor oil. Nevertheless, they prefer to avoid it as well if they have a choice.

To quench in motor oils, preheat the oil to anywhere between 200°F and 250°F.

Mineral Oil

Mineral oil is an alternative to motor oil. Its benefits are that it does not give off any odor, does not contain any harmful contaminants or toxins, and some of them are fairly odorless. If you can get your hands on high-grade mineral oil, then you might be able to avoid the flames that flare up during the quenching process.

In many cases, mineral oil is recommended for beginners.

To quench in mineral oil, preheat the oil to anywhere between 250°F and 300°F.

Baby Oil

Yes, you heard that right: baby oil. Many knifemakers head over to their local store and get a lot of baby oil for the process of quenching. Baby oil contains minimal contaminants, does not create flames easily, and tends to give rise to as little odor as possible. Should you prefer, you could even get yourself some scented baby oil. You can quench your blade and leave behind a nice fragrance as an extra-added bonus!

The downside to that is that you might require a fair amount of baby oil, and you might find yourself shelling out a fair bit of cash to acquire the right volume of oil for your project.

You can use the same preheating temperature for baby oil as you did for food oil, Aim for temperatures between 150°F and 200°F.

Quenching Oils

Finally, you can purchase special quenching oils for your project, taking advantage of the fact that you can find the right oil for a specific purpose. Working on a blade? You have a quenching oil for that. Working on an anvil? Sure, there is a quenching oil for that too. Need a specific quenching oil for a specific steel? Still, no problem.

Of course, with the number of options available to you, quenching oils might be a bit more expensive than other types of oils.

For quenching oils, the quenching temperature is unique to the type of oil you choose to purchase. The quenching temperature will be mentioned on the packaging, allowing you to not only have instructions for quenching but also to help you decide just what quenching oil you would like to use for your project.

One of the most popular fast quenching oils that you can find on the market is Parks 50.

## Forging Steel Colors

| Fahrenheit | The Color of the Steel | Process |
|---|---|---|
| 2,000° | Bright Yellow | Forging |
| 1,900° | Dark Yellow | Forging |

| | | |
|---|---|---|
| 1,800° | Orange Yellow | Forging |
| 1,700° | Orange | Forging |
| 1,600° | Orange Red | Forging |
| 1,500° | Bright Red | Forging |
| 1,400° | Red | Forging |
| 1,300° | Medium Red | - |
| 1,200° | Dull Red | - |
| 1,100° | Slight Red | - |
| 1,000° | Mostly Grey | - |
| 800° | Dark Grey | Tempering |
| 575° | Blue | Tempering |
| 540° | Dark Purple | Tempering |
| 520° | Purple | Tempering |
| 480° | Brown | Tempering |
| 445° | Light Straw | Tempering |

One of the things that you will notice when working with metals is that you usually aim for a color that is obvious enough as to exactly which color you are looking at. For example, if you heat the metal to orange, then the temperature of the metal is anywhere between 1,600 and 1,800°F. When you reach the temperature range, then you are good to proceed with the next step in the process.

# Chapter 10: Finishing the Knife

## Grinding

Grinding is the process of using files or sanding machines to shape the steel into forming a bevel.

Many people become concerned about the fact that the heat produced during grinding might affect the knife. This is not true. You can breathe a sigh of relief. The main reason for this is that you are typically grinding the knife before subjecting it to any form of heat treatment processes.

I understand that other bladesmiths prefer grinding after heat treatment. But in my opinion, doing it before heat treatment has less risks, especially when dealing with scrap steel.

There are many types of grinds that you can perform on your knife. But we are going to do a full flat grind on your knife. This guide has a few pointers on doing a flat grind on your knife. Let's get started.

1. The first thing that you are going to do is take out your knife and bring it close to the grinder. You should preferably use a fresh belt when you are grinding your knife so that it does not heat up the blade too much. The sequence of grits for the belts you should be using should be 36,60,120, and 220.

2. Do not press the blade too much towards the grind. Gently touch it and start moving the knife. This will allow the grind to make the shape of the edge on the knife.

3. Start the grind close to the edge and slowly make your way up to the spine. You will notice that the edge has a gradual and linear slope like shape to it now. Once you have worked on one side of the knife, flip it over.

4. Bring it close to the grind and then add the slope like shape on the other side as well.

## Making the Full Tang Knife Handle

A suitable piece of handle material must be chosen for this process. You can choose a natural material, usually an exotic wood, or a man-made material such as Micarta. We are using wood as the handle material in this set of instructions. The wood will need to be cut down the middle to make two halves. This can be done with the bandsaw or a handsaw. The handle design should be marked on the outer part of the scales, with a pencil to avoid confusion later. It is important that the grain of the wood lines up as it did before it was cut. The inside cuts are ground smooth and flat with one of the belt sanders.

The forward edge of one of the handle pieces is ground square and then held against the guard and viewed in the light. If there are any gaps in the guard/handle joint, they will be visible when examined in the light.

1. Cut off the handle material to close to the shape of your markings carefully. You are doing this because you want the material to match the tang design of the knife.

2. Clamp together the scales and the tang before drilling, so that the holes are in line.

3. Drill the holes into the tang as marked by the pencil design. Then cut out rivets or use Corby fasteners as pins for the handle. Hammer them in place inside the holes and make sure they fit tight.

4. Rub the scales using acetone to remove any moisture from them.

5. Clean the tang and guard with acetone to remove any oils or dirt, and then mix some epoxy. The first side of handle material is carefully glued and clamped in place, making sure that the handle joint is tight. Once the glue has set, the pinholes are hammered through the handle from the side of the tang. If the handle material does not follow the profile of the tang, just take a bit of time to cut it closer to the final dimensions.

6. If there is too much epoxy, then you have to make sure that it gets cleaned off to allow it to attach sufficiently the other side of the handle. The forward end of the remaining handle piece is mated to the guard using the light to determine needed adjustments. Then the exposed tang is cleaned again with acetone, new epoxy is mixed, and the remaining handle is glued to the knife.

7. The handle is now shaped using the belt sander. Pinholes are left open until the handle is sanded to #120 grit. Then the pins are applied a little bit of epoxy and added, peened in place if necessary and grounded flush with the handle.

## Sharpening

Sharpening the edge of your blade is the last step in making your knife. Like most things in knifemaking, every maker has their preferred method for sharpening. You should ideally look for a sharpening process where you are able to use the knife effectively for your lifestyle and needs.

So how to sharpen the blade?

There are many ways but here are some that might be useful for you.

Apart from the sharpeners mentioned in the list below, you can also use the Lansky Knife Sharpening System. The Lansky is a complete kit for sharpening that is ideal for beginners.

## V Sharpener

These sharpening tools have two edges, shaped in a V. A blade can be moved through the V with light pressure to grind the edge. By holding the sharpeners at a specific angle, it creates consistency in every pass that can be hard to obtain using a stone. Unfortunately, it most likely isn't the exact angle you want. It also won't compensate for the loss of steel that occurs with use over time and will change the shape of your edge.

## Waterstones

Waterstones require water to be used as a lubricant. One of the things you might notice when using them is that their surface keeps wearing away. This exposes new layers and makes them great for sharpening. You can also use this stone to polish the bevel. The constant wear creates an indentation in the top of the stone, which needs to be flattened frequently to maintain a good surface for grinding. The waterstone is an option that is recommended for beginners. It allows beginners to easily grasp the basics of sharpening.

## Belt Grinder

Belt grinders are one of the most popular forms of sharpeners and as you might have noticed, we have used the grinding process liberally throughout this book. Basically, the same grinder that you used to make your grinds can be used to sharpen your edge. The knife is held gently at the appropriate angle against the slack part of a fine belt. Doing this takes a good eye and a steady hand and can be difficult for a beginner due to the speed at which the metal is removed. Grinding in this manner tends to create a slightly convex grind.

## Taking Care of Your Knife

After you have invested a lot of time into your blade, it would be a shame if you were to ruin it too quickly.

So here are a few notes that you should remember about knife care.

Those who make knives are at an advantage when it comes to knowing how to take care of a blade. Now that you know what it takes to make your blade, it's easier to focus on avoiding the situations that what will ruin one. If you find yourself in a survival scenario, it's incredibly vital to protect the knife that you are going to use to keep you alive. Even if you are not, it can be harmful to ruin something you have taken so much time to create.

One of the things that ruin the knife quicker is when people place it in the dirt whenever they are outside. The idea behind that is that they can easily reach for their knives when they have to. But this does not do anything except dull the blade of the knife even further. Of course, it does look cool in the movies when the actor does it. But when have we ever used movies as a guide to real life situations?

Avoid using any cutting surface that is as hard as your blade's edge. Some people try and use a rock as a cutting surface. Don't do that. Your blade will be grateful to you if you use a log or piece of wood instead. Cutting boards not only serve as a surface to cut on, but also are also important to protect the integrity of the knife.

Make sure to dry your blade when it gets wet and to rinse it if it comes into contact with saltwater. Don't store your blade for long periods of time in the sheath, as the leather can collect moisture and cause corrosion.

All carbon steel will need care to prevent corrosion in the form of surface rust, so anything you can do to be proactive is a big help. If you do see rust forming, use fine grit paper to remove it as soon as possible and apply a light coat of oil.

You can also get a patina on the knife instead of rust. Now the line of difference between a patina and rust is very thin as they might almost look similar. However, patina is more controlled whereas rust can spread easily. In order to create a patina, simply dip your blade into boiling water. This oxidizes the rust and you have a fine layer of patina on your knife.

# Conclusion

Forging is not difficult.

However, for many of the processes, the results won't be instant. You have to slowly work your way to getting the desired results.

And that is where more people fail. That is what makes forging difficult; it is not the idea that people can't get something done, but the fact that they can't get it done instantly. It is a laboring process and it does tax your body as well.

However, remember that as long as you make sure that you are taking precautions at all times to protect yourself, work with the instructions you have, then you won't have to worry about anything.

With that, I hope you enjoy forging and creating your own very fine blade.

# References

Hrisoulas, J. (2010). *Master bladesmith*. Boulder, Colo.: Paladin.

Hrisoulas, J. (2017). *Pattern-Welded Blade*. NEPHILIM Press.

Hrisoulas, J., Morris, J. and Sherbring, M. (2017). *The complete bladesmith*. Redd Ink Press.

Sims, L. (2009). *The backyard blacksmith*. Crestline Books.

# Heat Treatment Secrets for Bladesmithing

# Introduction

Steel has more than 95% iron with trace amounts of Carbon.

Why is this important? It is because pure iron is a comparatively soft element that can easily rust. On the other hand, with the right alloy, it turns into a material that is difficult to bend.

Steel can be made to be strong, more solid than iron, and resistant to corrosives. It is also a versatile material, which you can use to make objects ranging from your everyday kitchen utensils and tools to office appliances to automobile parts, building materials, and machinery.

But you might be curious; aren't there any materials better than steel? There are. For example, carbon fiber, made from thin sheets of carbon, is considered to be more durable, flexible, heat and electricity resistant, and stronger than steel. However, it cannot be used more than steel. That is because of the availability of materials.

You see, among all the metals that we currently know of, iron is the second most naturally abundant material found on Earth after aluminum. About 4.7% of the Earth's crust is made up of iron and it appears as different types of oxides. The main product that iron is used to manufacture is, you guessed it, steel.

Apart from the easy access to iron, one of the things that makes steel important in today's manufacturing and construction landscape is the fact that steel can be recycled easily. In fact, the American Iron and Steel Institute has discovered that nearly 88% of steel is recycled in many parts of the world. One of the more spectacular aspects of recycling steel is its ability to retain some of its properties. If you start recycling other materials, they begin to lose their strength after each recycle. But not steel. Even after recycling multiple times, steel does not lose its integrity and strength. This feature also becomes important for the simple fact that you do not see a lot of wastage when it comes to steel.

So what does this have to do with bladesmithing?

Simple, you are working on one of the most magnificent materials known to man. When you apply heat treatment to this material, you are not destroying its strength. You are not causing it to rust. You are not deteriorating its quality.

You are making use of its advantages to make some incredible tools for yourself.


Heat treatment is a simple but effective technique that prevents your blade from shattering.

However, before we get down to working with steel, it is important to know just what exactly we are doing.

# Chapter 1: Iron Management

## It's Gettin' Hot in Here! What is Heat Treatment?

Essentially, no material or finished product can be manufactured without sending it through the process of heat treating. In this process, a particular metal is heated to a high temperature and then cooled under specific conditions to improve its characteristics, stability, and performance.

Through heat treatment, you can soften a metal, which allows the metal to become more flexible. You can also use heat treatment to harden metals, ensuring that their strength is improved.

In fact, heat treatment is essential if you are in the business of manufacturing parts for automobiles, aircraft, computers, and other forms of heavy machinery and tools. In other words, if you want something important built, then you need to subject the material to heat treatment.

Iron, and more specifically steel, are the most common materials that go through heat treatment. However, that does not mean that other materials cannot be treated with heat.

It has been estimated that heat treatment adds more than $10 billion in value to materials by enhancing their durability and quality.

In short, this process is quite important and you are going to learn to use it.

## Temper Tantrums

One of the processes of heat treatment is called tempering. In this process, you are basically altering the mechanical attributes (usually the flexibility and strength) of steel or products and items made from steel. Tempering releases the carbon molecules confined in the steel to diffuse from martensite. Martensite is a form of a crystalline structure consisting of brittle carbon that exists in hardened steel. Because of martensite's features, the steel may be hard, but it also becomes brittle, rendering it useless in most applications.

It then allows the internal stresses that may have been formed due to past uses to be discharged from the steel. This results in the alloy becoming more durable.

So how does one temper their steel? Firstly, the steel is heated to a high temperature, but it is not allowed to heat up beyond its melting point. Once that is done, it is then cooled in air. There is no fixed temperature for all forms of steel. They each have their own temperature range that must be reached first. Alternatively, temperatures can also be adjusted to fit the degree of hardness one would like to reduce in the steel.

For example, when you heat the steel at low temperatures, then you are reducing the brittleness in the material and increasing the hardness. This could be applicable for certain purposes, such as setting the steel.

Other times, the steel is heated at high temperatures. When this is done, it reduces the toughness of the metal but then increases its flexibility. This is useful when you would like to work further on the metal.

When you temper the metal, it is important to heat the metal gradually until it reaches the temperature you would like to work with. This prevents the metal from cracking.

## Annealing

Annealing is another process similar to heat treatment, focused on softening the metal or reducing the hardness of the material. We usually use this process after subjecting the material to a softening or hardening treatment. Through annealing, you are trying to return materials to a state before they were cooled. This allows you to reshape them or form them in a particular manner with relative ease.

When metals are subjected to cold treatment, they could become so hard that if you perform any more work on them, they might begin to crack. Obviously, that is not something we would like to achieve. When you perform the process of annealing before you subject the metal to cold treatment, then you reduce the chances of cracking the metal.

Typically, you might discover that annealing takes place in large ovens. The space inside the over must be large enough that when the metallic object is placed inside, there is still room for proper air circulation around the metal.

When you cool materials, their degree of malleability reduces. Their strength goes up and it becomes difficult to work on them again. When you use annealing, you are giving yourself the opportunity to perform modifications on the material, should you require it.

In this process, the metal is heated to a temperate where it is possible to attain recrystallization. This means that new non-deformed grains take over the positions of the deformed grains. And what exactly are grains? In metallurgy, each grain is a single crystal that consists of a specific arrangement of atoms. When you have deformed grains, then you cannot work on the metal without causing more deformity. In this case, the deformity appears in the form of cracks. When you perform the annealing process, you are forming new grains, which means you are giving yourself the ability to work on the metal again.

## Quenching

This is a pretty popular process in metallurgy and you might have seen it being performed on TV or in the movies. Quenching is an essential step for heat treatment. Without it, the other steps are rather futile. Basically, the metal worker takes the steel and then dips it into a cauldron, often creating a dramatic effect. You can see steam rising and the water sizzling as the metal cools. However, water is not the only medium that the metal worker uses for the process of quenching. Before we dive into that, let us look at the quenching process in more detail.

Quenching is a process that occurs after another process where the metal is heated to high temperatures. Examples of the kind of processes that precede quenching are annealing (which we looked at earlier) or normalizing (which we shall look at in the next section). In both annealing and normalizing, the cooling process can take some time. This could affect the strength of the steel, causing it to lower more than necessary. Through quenching, you are lowering the temperature considerably, which could benefit the work that you are doing. Metal workers usually apply this method so that they can prevent the cooling process from altering the molecular structure of the metal.

Quenching is typically done by subjecting the metal immediately to a certain liquid, typically water, or to forced air. In a forced air cooling system, the air is pushed out through specially arranged ducts that help in, you guessed it, cooling the temperature of an object quickly. The water or air used for the process of quenching is termed the "medium."

But you have to be careful not to plunge the hot steel into the medium too quickly, it can ruin the quality of your heat treat. This is a huge mistake that you have to avoid.

Another warning, never use a plastic container to store your quenching medium. Doing so is a sure-fire method to start a fire in your workshop.

Now you might think to yourself - is there any other liquid that can be used for quenching? That is a valid point actually. We are so used to seeing the movies show metallic objects such as swords and weapons being dipped into water that we are not aware of any other liquids that can be used. However, here a couple of other liquids that are used for quenching:

## Oil

There are numerous oil options that you can use for the process of quenching. You have fish oils, vegetable oils, and certain mineral oils that can help you attain the desired effect. With each medium, you have a different rate of cooling. When you use oil, you are using a liquid that has a higher cooling rate than air but cools the metal down more slowly than water.

When choosing oils, here are a few options that you can consider for your bladesmithing requirements:

### Food Grade Oils

Many bladesmiths and knife makers utilize food grade oils for the sole reason that they are cheaper and readily available. You can head over to your local supermarket or store and find one on their shelves. In fact, you are also spoilt for choice, with the number of different brands available to you. A famous food oil used in quenching is canola oil.

Canola oil is very easy to find. Just a visit to your grocery store will be enough. It also reduces the chances of your steel cracking while you quench it, as it doesn't allow your steel to cool too quickly.

During the quenching and tempering processes, food oils spread a much more bearable odor than other types of oil. While you might think that this is a minor point to make note of, it might affect you if you have a workshop attached to your home or within your home.

To quench in food grade oils, preheat the oil to anywhere between 150°F to 200°F.

## Motor Oil

Another oil that is popularly used in the knife-making industry or hobby is motor oil. People use both new and used motor oil, depending on their requirements. The advantage of motor oil is that it is really cheap to obtain. In fact, used motor oil is free; you may have it in your garage, you might find some in your friend's garage or even in the local store.

However, do note that used motor oil tends to leave a stench. Additionally, you might find a dark film that coats the blade you are working on which is quite difficult to remove. Another reason why you might want to stay away from used motor oil is the fact that they contain quite a few toxins that could be potentially harmful when inhaled. For beginners, it is highly recommended that they do not use motor oils. Experienced knife makers who have worked with the blade for many years might be able to spot a good motor oil. Nevertheless, they prefer to avoid it as well if they have a choice.

To quench in motor oils, preheat the oil to anywhere between 200°F to 250°F.

## Mineral Oil

Mineral oil is an alternative to motor oil. Their benefit is that they do not give off any odor, do not contain any harmful contaminants or toxins, and some of them are fairly odorless. If you can get your hands on high-grade mineral oil, then you might be able to avoid the flames that flare up during the quenching process.

In many cases, mineral oil is recommended for beginners.

To quench in mineral oil, preheat the oil to anywhere between 250°F to 300°F.

## Baby Oil

You heard that right. Many knife makers head over to their local store and get a lot of baby oil for the process of quenching. Baby oil contains minimal contaminants, does not create flames easily, and tends to give rise to as little odor as possible. Should you prefer, you could even get yourself a scented baby oil. You can quench your blade and leave behind a nice smell as a bonus!

The downside is that, as you might require a fair amount of baby oil, you might find yourself shelling out a bit of cash to acquire the right volume of oil for your project.

You can use the same preheating temperature for baby oil as you did for food oil, between 150°F to 200°F.

## Quenching Oils

Finally, you can purchase special quenching oils for your project, taking advantage of the fact that you can find the right oil for a specific purpose. Working on a blade? You have a quenching oil for that. Working on an anvil? Sure, there is a quenching oil for that. Need a specific quenching oil for a specific steel? Sure, no problem.

Of course, with the number of options available to you, quenching oils might be a bit more expensive than other forms of oils.

For quenching oils, the quenching temperature is unique to the type of oil you choose to purchase. The quenching temperature will be mentioned on the packaging, allowing you to not only have instructions for quenching but also to help you decide just what quenching oil you would like to use for your project.

## Brine

When you dissolve rock salts in water, then the result is a liquid called brine. What is so special about this brine? It lowers the concentration of atmospheric gases. This, in turn, lowers the number of bubbles formed during the quenching process. The result is that brine cools the metal faster than water can.

Here is a key point to remember about quenching. You need to use the medium that best suits your purpose. Different kinds of steel might require different periods of cooling, even though your main aim is to cool them as fast as possible.

When you want to quench in brine, you typically keep the temperature between 150°F to 200°F. However, in some cases you can bring the temperature to around 100°F as well, depending on the steel.

Having understood the different kinds of oils, a few people often ask, "Is there a method of quenching that is ideal for the metal?" As a matter of fact, there is. When you are quenching, make sure that you move the blade forward and backward in the liquid, almost as though you are poking something. This will allow the metal to cool faster.

## Normalizing

During normalizing, you are refining the size of the grain in the metal. Should you need a refresher course on what grains are, you can always refer to the section on annealing. After normalizing, the mechanical properties of the metal are improved.

Normalizing sets a uniformity to the structure of grains in the metal. After you have achieved uniformity, you have reduced the degree of deformity of the metal. This allows you to get an even finish and a wonderful product in the end.

In the process of normalizing, steel is heated to a really high temperature and then cooled by leaving the metal at room temperature. This process of rapidly heating up the metal and then slowly cooling it down makes changes in the microstructure of the metal, making it elastic and durable. Normalizing is almost like a process of correction. This is because it is typically used when some other process unintentionally increases the hardness but decreases the malleability of the metal. What makes normalizing different from other processes such as annealing is that it uses room temperature to cool down the metal, rather than any medium or special technique.

We all know the basic property of heat; it expands. This is practically what happens to metals as well. The heat causes them to expand. It also affects the structure, magnetism, and electrical resistance of the metal. What you are doing is making sure that the metal turns out just the way you want it to. The temperature to which you heat the metal and then the temperature to which you cool the metal affects the overall properties of the metal. As seen above, we can affect the metal's hardness, malleability, ductility, and even its resistance to corrosion by using the right heat treatment.

# Chapter 2: Real Steel

In this chapter, we are looking at the properties and temperatures of the various types of steel you will be working with. We are going to deal with as many details as possible for each of the steel variations. So let us start with the first one.

## 1080 steel

1080 is part of a series of steels that are known as carbon steels. They are called so because these variations of steel possess carbon as the principal alloying element. Now do not confuse alloying element with the primary element (also known as the base element). As we pointed out before, the base element in steel is iron. That does not change. Alloying elements refer to those materials that combine with the base material to form an alloy.

In addition to carbon, this series of steel also has trace amounts of silicon (0.4%) and manganese (1.2%). You might also find small quantities of other elements such as molybdenum, chromium, copper, nickel, and aluminum. This form of steel has one of the highest electrical conductivities among molded carbon or non-alloy forms of metal. In addition, it has comparatively low ductility. In some cases, you might also find this metal to have a moderately high tensile strength. The below information will allow you to understand more about 1080 carbon steel in detail.

## Chemical Composition

The main elements present in 1080 steel are highlighted below;

Iron - around 98%

Carbon - around 0.80%

Manganese - around 0.60% to 0.90%

Sulfur - a maximum of 0.05%

Phosphorous - a maximum of 0.04%

## Mechanical Properties

Elastic modulus - 190-210 GPa

Let us try to understand what elastic modulus really means. Have you ever stretched a spring? You might have tried to pull it to its maximum length and then let go. Typically, the spring bounces back to its original position. However, if you were to keep stretching the spring, then you would reach a point where the spring will not return to its original form. This property of elasticity holds for many materials, including steel.

When you apply a certain amount of force to a material, then you stretch the material. When you remove the application of force, then the material returns to its original shape. However, there is always a limit to the amount of force you can apply to stretch a material. The ratio of strain that an object can handle because of its elasticity is called the elastic modulus of the material.

Poisson's ratio - 0.27 to 0.30

When a material stretches, it does so in two different directions. If we were to take the example of the spring, then upon stretching it, it increases in length but decreases in diameter. The increase in the length is known as the longitudinal strain and any changes to the diameter or width of the material are referred to as the lateral strain.

It is this change in the lateral strain and longitudinal strain that you denote using Poisson's ratio.

Additionally, carbon steel is also available in two different formats.

You have carbon steel that is hot rolled and you have carbon steel that is cold drawn. Let us look at the difference between the two.

## 1095 Steel

Once again, 1095 steel forms a part of the carbon steel series. This means that carbon is the major allowing steel here once again. Here are the properties of 1095 steel.

## Chemical Composition

Iron - around 98%

Carbon - around 1.03%

Sulfur - less than or exactly 0.050%

Phosphorous - less than or exactly 0.040%

Manganese - less than or exactly 0.50%

## Physical Properties of 1095 steel

Density - 7.85 g/cm³

Melting point - 2759°F (1515°C)

# Mechanical Properties

Tensile strength - 685 MPa

When you use the term tensile strength, then you are referring to the degree to which a material can stretch before it will break or fail. Now, tensile is different from elastic modulus because it does not measure the rate at which a material can bounce back to its original position after stretching.

The final tensile strength of a metal is measured by taking the area of the material, which is also the cross-section of the metal. You then divide it by the stress exerted on the metal. The stress that metal bears is typically represented as pounds or tons per square inch of metal. The tensile strength of a metal is an important measurement. This is because it looks at a metal's ability to function in various applications. It is a widely used measurement for metals and alloys, so it would be prudent to make a note of it when working with various metals.

Yield strength - 525 MPa

Elastic modulus - around 210 GPa

Poisson's ratio - around 0.30

## 15N20 Steel

As you are making blades, 15N20 is an incredible steel for the purpose. What makes it a standout steel is the fact that it is tough and allows you to subject it to heat treatment easily. One of its more common uses is to make the bandsaw blades that are commonly found in sawmills.

One of the remarkable things about 15N20 is that it can be used as a blade material on its own. However, should you choose to, you can mix with other steel materials in pattern welded damascus.

Now you might be thinking. What exactly is damascus? Well, when you make steel products with a wavy pattern on the surface, then you have a damascus steel. You can achieve this form of steel by using a hammer to weld strips of iron and steel. Then you have to subject both metals to repeated forging and heat treatment processes. Damascus steel is used mainly for the purpose of making blades for knives and swords. We will look at a popular combination of damascus steel further down below.

As nickel is also present in 15N20, it provides a nice contrast to the steel, giving it a wonderful aesthetic appearance. Once you have made the blade with 15N20 steel, it also becomes easy to sharpen. You can create a really fine edge with the steel and also make it tough.

Apart from the above, nickel has many uses when it is present in the steel.

## Chemical Composition

Iron - approximately 97%

Carbon - approximately 0.75%

Manganese - a maximum of 0.4%

Nickel - approximately 2.0%

## O1 Steel

There are certain types of steels known as cold-work steels. These are high carbon steels and typically appear in three categories. These categories are:

- Oil-hardening steels

- High-carbon and high-chromium steels

- Air-hardening steels.

Among the three of the aforementioned steels, we are going to focus on oil-hardening steels. These are also known as O steels and come in various forms. The one that we shall be working with will be O1. So let us look at what this steel is made of.

O1 steel's main composition consists of metals such as chromium, manganese, and tungsten, and is relatively inexpensive. The following datasheet provides details about O1 type steel. Now, we already know that iron is the major component in steel, so let us try and understand what other elements we are going to be dealing with in O1 steel.

## Chemical Composition

Carbon - around 1%

Manganese - around 1.4%

Silicon - around 0.40%

Chromium - around 0.60%

Nickel - 0.30%

Tungsten - around 0.60%

Vanadium - 0.30%

Copper - 0.25%

Phosphorous - 0.03%

Sulfur - 0.03%

We can see that O1 has a fair mixture of alloys, with even sulfur and phosphorous coming into the mix. Now it is time to look at some of the mechanical properties and understand a new term present in the measurement.

## Mechanical Properties

Density (hardened to 62 HRC) - 7.81 g/cm³

HRC refers to the Rockwell Hardness of a particular steel. When you are using this term, then the higher the Rockwell hardness number, the stronger the steel. A lower number means that the steel is fairly malleable. With a measurement of 62 HRC, we can see that O1 is fairly strong. If the number were to dip to a level of, say, 32 HRC, then we are looking at a weaker metal which is malleable to work with.

Melting point - 2590°F (around 1421°C)

## Damascus Steel

We use "Damascus Steel" to indicate two forms of ferrous materials (those materials that contain iron). These materials can easily be identified by the unique pattern present on them which is produced as a result of a controlled combination of steel and iron. One of the common forms of Damascus Steel includes a combination of 1095 and 15N20 steel. As we saw earlier, 1095 steel is a high-carbon steel, giving you great strength that you can use for your blade. 15N20 steel, on the other hand, allows you to heat treat it really well. When you combine the two, you get a strong and superb blade. Additionally, with 1095 steel's properties, your Damascus blade will be highly resistant to wear over time and after repeated use.

## Chemical Properties

Iron - around 97.5%

Carbon - around 0.98%

Manganese - around 0.45%

Sulfur - less than 0.050%

Phosphorous - less than 0.040%

## Mechanical Properties

Yield Strength - 485 MPa

Elongation (the degree to which you can extend the length of the blade) - 3.2%.

To understand this, measure 3.2% of the original blade length. That is the maximum additional length you can add to the Damascus steel blade made from 1095 and 15N20 steel when you are extending it.

## Stainless steel

Some of the main advantages of stainless steel might not be obvious. However, when you begin to compare it to other forms of steel, such as plain carbon steel, then the advantages start to become apparent. There are many properties that govern stainless steel. However, the main features that set it apart are:

- High cryogenic toughness

- High work hardening rate

- Low maintenance

- High hardness and strength

- High corrosion resistance

- High ductility

- More attractive appearance

At a molecular level, stainless steel is mainly an iron-based alloy. It also contains a minimum composition of around 10% of chromium. The presence of chromium adds an interesting effect to the entire combination. The chromium adds a protective oxide layer that is also self-healing. It is this layer that confers corrosion resistance to stainless steel. What does the presence of this self-healing feature mean?

Well, stainless steel can essentially retain its corrosive resistance no matter what fabrication methods you use. This means that despite the work you perform, the healing properties of the chromium layer can always be found in the end product. In fact, even if you damaged the surface while working on it, you will not remove the corrosion resistance abilities of the steel. It will always be there.

Additionally, you might also find that stainless steel has a high cryogenic resistance. This type of resistance is characterized by the fact that the blade or steel retains its toughness at sub-zero temperatures.

Stainless steel also has hot strength. What does this mean? Hot strength is the ability of the steel or blade to retain its toughness at high temperatures. The high levels of chromium allow the steel to have this form of toughness as well.

You may find stainless steels in various forms. Let us look at a few of them.

## Austenitic Stainless Steels

These forms of steel are unique because they feature around 6% nickel and more than 16% chromium. They might also contain elements such as molybdenum.

When you include more elements such as molybdenum or even copper in some cases, then you can change the properties of the steel. The type of element used can provide a specific type of property. You can make the steel suitable for dealing with high temperatures or heighten its corrosive resistance. The type of property depends on what you want out of your product.

Additionally, many forms of steel become weak when they are subjected to low temperatures. With the presence of nickel in austenitic stainless allows the metal to retain its strength at low temperatures.

Some of the products that austenitic stainless steel is used in are shown below:

Roofing and gutters

Kitchen sinks

Ovens

Chemical tanks

Doors and windows

## Martensitic Stainless Steels

With these kinds of steel, what you are getting is a metal with lower chromium content as compared to other forms of stainless steel. However, you also receive a comparatively higher carbon content.

Some of the products that utilize martensitic stainless steel are noted down below:

Knife blades

Springs

Cutlery

Surgical instruments

Fasteners

## Ferritic Stainless Steels

What makes this kind of stainless steel unique is that the major alloying element in them is only chromium. No other elements make a large contribution to the metal as an alloy. The amount of chromium that is present varies between different ferritic stainless steels. Typically, you might find a quantity that ranges anywhere from 10% to 18%. This increases their resistance to cracking from stress corrosion.

Some of the applications in which you might find the use of ferratic stainless steels are:

Fuel lines

Vehicle exhausts

Domestic appliances

Cooking utensils

## Duplex Stainless Steels

With duplex stainless steels, you might discover that they include a low percentage of nickel and higher traces of chromium. With the percentages mentioned above, duplex stainless steel features microstructures that give it a close resemblance to both austenitic and ferritic types of steel. The common form of alloy composition in duplex stainless steel includes roughly 23% chromium and around 4% nickel. Alternatively, you can also find close to 22% chromium and around 5% nickel compositions of this steel.

Some of the applications that utilize duplex stainless steel are:

Marine applications

Heat exchangers

Offshore oil & gas installations

Desalination plants

## Scrap Steel

Most of us know how to recycle various objects including everyday items like plastic bottles, newspapers, wood and other materials. However, there are many ways in which you can recycle steel as well. The method which is most important to us is in the use of knife making (of course)!

You may find different types of scrap steels. Here are a few common steel scraps that you can get your hands on and their chemical composition:

### Leaf Springs

*Chemical Composition*

Iron - about 98%

Carbon - less than or equal to 0.5%

Silicon - less than or equal to 0.7%

Manganese - around 0.7%

Sulfur - a maximum of 0.05%

## Steel Tubes

*Chemical Composition*

Iron - about 97.5%

Carbon - anywhere from 0.55% to 0.75%

Manganese - around 0.6%

Sulfur - a maximum of 0.035%

Copper - around 0.2%

Chromium - around 0.15%

Molybdenum - around 0.06%

Nickel - less than or equal to 0.20%

## Surgical Stainless Steel Items

*Chemical Composition*

Iron - around 98%

Carbon - around 0.5%

Chromium - around 0.05%

Nickel - less than or equal to 0.2%

Molybdenum - less than or equal to 0.05%

Silicon - less than or equal to 0.04%

Aluminum - no more than 0.025%

## Saw Blades

*Chemical Composition*

Iron - around 98%

Carbon - anywhere from 0.7% to 0.8%

Manganese - around 0.4%

Sulfur - a maximum of 0.05%

Phosphorous - a maximum of 0.04%

**Steel Rebar**

*Chemical Composition*

Iron - anywhere from 98.4% to 98.9%

Manganese - anywhere from 0.75% to 1.05%

Sulfur - anywhere from 0.26% to 0.35%

Carbon - around 0.09%

Phosphorous - anywhere from 0.040% to 0.090%

# Chapter 3: Working With the Metals

Now we are going to focus on how you can work with each of these materials. Now, what essentially happens is that you must first harden the blade and then temper it properly in order for you to generate the desired product that will be useful for its intended function.

The procedure you have to follow for heat-treating a blade is fairly easy: you have to heat the blade to the right temperature, then you quench it using the correct medium, and then temper the hardness into the metal to a point where is not brittle anymore. That does sound easy enough. Excited to get your metal under heat treatment?

Before you try to harden the steel, identify the type of steel you are using to create the blade and what the hardening temperature of the blade is. Being informed about your alloy's tempering and hardening temperatures is the most essential part of the tempering and hardening process. Do note that if you would like to try out using steel, then you can work with scrap steel before moving on to other forms of steel. We shall cover working with scrap steel further down in the chapter.

During many stages of heat treatment, you can perform any machining or grinding processes that you may want to do. Machining is the process of cutting material to transform it into certain shapes based on your preference. Grinding is another process of adding shape to your material, but this time, you utilize a grinding wheel to make cuts into the metal. You can use any of these processes to create a blade that fits your idea, so now would be a good time to add a little creativity to your work!

When you are producing a blade, one of the most important steps that you will encounter is grinding. Once you have properly ground a blade, you will have an uninterrupted edge that will have little to no flaws. Of course, mastering the grinding technique requires a lot of patience and perhaps more than a few trials and errors. Since grinding is an essential step in bladesmithing, let us look at a few ways to perform the grinding method.

## The Hollow Ground Edge

The hollow ground edge has a concave edge. This form of an edge is well suited to blades that will be mainly used for slicing. Examples of such blades include skinners, hunters, filet knives, etc.

The main reason why the hollow ground edge is suitable for such knives is the fact that it produces a very thin edge that can be sharpened quite easily. However, because of this thin edge, the blade can be rather fragile as compared to other forms of grinds. This is why it is not prudent to simply make a hollow ground edge if you are going to be using your blade against heavier substances such as bone, wood, or substances with similar thickness. An important fact to know here is most of the blades produced around the world today are hollow ground. It could be because not many people are looking to cut bone or thicker materials!

Another feature of the hollow ground to note is that it produces a strong and light blade that adopts a sharp edge easily.

Here is how you can achieve a hollow grind.

Step 1: You are going to use a grinding wheel or a belt for a hollow grind.

Step 2: Take the blade and slowly bring the edge to the surface of the wheel of the belt.

Step 3: Now start the wheel of the belt and allow for the grind to form. For beginners, getting the perfect grind might not be easy. However, with practice you should be able to get the edge that you require.

## The Cannel Edge

The cannel edge is also known as the "appleseed" edge. It is a superb option to make an edge for heavy-chopping blades such as cleavers, axes, and anything else that will be used to cut through numerous thick objects such as bones and wood. The cannel ground makes a fairly strong edge and will remain steady for a long time. You might find that the edge is rugged as the edge also features numerous cross-sections. These cross sections can cause the sword to be fairly heavy when you are done working on the blade. Additionally, it is not a difficult edge for you to master. You just have to understand the concept that the entire blade will have a smooth, rounded surface. Once you become aware of this, you will know how to work with the blade and what to do with the grind.

Step 1: Note that this is one of the most challenging edges to master so you should only approach this edge grind if you are confident in your ability to produce it. With just a single mistake, you could ruin your blade entirely. For this grind, you will require a slack-flat belt grinder. This is not a grinder commonly used by hobbyists. Only professionals or industries make use of this grinder.

Step 2: Bring the edge to the surface of the grinder.

Step 3: As the grind is being made, you need to move the blade from the edge to the spine. Essentially, you are creating a convex blade shape that starts sharp near the blade's edge and broadens as you reach the spine.

Step 4: Take sandpaper and use backward strokes (stroking the knife from spine to edge) to perfect the convex shape of your blade. Do note that the longer the blade, the more sandpaper you will require.

## The Flat Grind

The flat grind creates a nice balance between the hollow grind and the cannel grind. One of the main advantages it provides is that, since it draws from both the hollow grind and the cannel grind, it has an excellent edge that can bear the brunt of heavy chopping. Additionally, even after multiple chopping sessions, it can still retain its sharpness. However, its main disadvantage is that it is one of the trickier grinding methods to work with so it may take some time to learn.

Step 1: The flat grind is similar to the hollow grind but is simpler to perform. This is because you are not focusing on the edge alone, but on the entire blade.

Step 2: Your technique involves a process similar to the hollow grind. Bring the edge close to the grinding wheel or belt.

Step 3: When the edge is sharp, continue working on the blade all the way to the spine.

Step: Once you are done, you should notice a linear slope that starts from the edge and goes all the way to the spine.

## The Chisel Edge

Some parts of the world use this edge mainly to create various forms of knives. However, in other areas, some of the more common products that feature this edge include carpenter's axes and wood chisels. The chisel edge is a special edge made for a specific reason; it makes the blade sturdy. The chisel edge best fits the manufacturing of tools and utensils.

Step 1: The chisel grind is another easy grind to perform on your blade. The main reason for this is that the blade is flat on one side but has a grind on the other. Start off by bringing one edge of your blade close to the grinding wheel or belt.

Step 2: Do note that you can bring any edge to the blade. Then you follow the same steps as required for the hollow edge. In fact, you can think of the chisel edge as a single-sided hollow edge.

Step 3: Do not worry about how the flat side looks. You do not have to grind the edge in such a way that it appears symmetrical to the other side. This is because there is no edge on the other side to match your grind. Simply grind the edge and sharpen it. The angle of the bevel is entirely up to you and the aesthetic you would like to add to your blade.

## Working with 1080

1080 has a somewhat higher manganese composition than other carbon steels in the 10XX category. Because it is a relatively easy steel to work with, it makes 1080 an ideal steel for beginners who want to start their bladesmithing adventure. It gives you enough room to make errors when it comes to heat treatment. It is known to form an almost complete pearlite structure when you subject it to annealing and normalizing processes. Pearlite is a form of structure that features alternating layers. Because of this arrangement of layers, it is easily considered to be one of the strongest material structures on this planet.

Additionally, 1080 contains nearly 0.80% carbon (which is represented by the 80 in 1080) and is known to produce a good quality knife with a nice edge.

Now comes the rest of the process.

## Annealing

In the annealing process, you start off by heating the metal to 1500°F. Then you have to cool the metal but you should avoid cooling it too quickly. You have to ensure that the metal cools at a rate of 50°F per hour or lower. I would not recommend going below 45°F for this purpose.

PRO TIP: In many cases, knife makers use an overnight cooling strategy. For this, you heat the metal to the required temperature of 1500°F at the end of the day. Ensure that the last heat of the day is slowly disappearing by the time you remove the metal from the forge. Once that is done, you then cool the metal in the forge overnight. This becomes handy when you have to perform other work or you might be engaged in the evening.

At this point, you can perform your machining or grinding process, should you wish to.

## Normalizing

For the normalizing process, you heat the metal to 1600°F in a forge. You can also raise the heat to a high temperature of around 2150°F. Do not attempt to work on the metal below 1500°F. Once the temperature has been reached, quench the metal for about four minutes. For the right quenching liquid, I have provided a recommendation below.

After four minutes, allow the metal to cool in still air. When you normalize the steel, you are resetting the crystalline structure. Through this reset, you are distributing the carbides in such a manner that they become uniform.

When you are working with steel, having an uneven structure affects its quality. Which is why, if you do not reset the structure, the carbides tend to group together tightly. Due to this, the steel will not have the sharp uniform edge that it could have had.

## Quenching

For the process of quenching, you should ideally invest in a fast quench oil. These are special oils that you can use for working with 1080 steel. You need to ensure that the 1080 steel is at 900°F before you introduce it to the quenching process.

PRO TIP: Preheat the oil beforehand. You will be able to cool your steel faster.

# Hardening

Your next mission, should you choose to accept it (I recommend you do to get the best results) is hardening the metal. For this, you heat the steel to 1500°F. You are aiming to push it past its non-magnetic limit. In this case, that limit is around 1425°F.

When you are working in the forge, you have to heat the metal until the metal does not attract a magnet to itself. When you have reached such a state, you heat it to a slightly higher temperature. This is just to make sure that you have truly pushed the steel into the non-magnetic area.

If you overheat the steel by keeping it at temperatures of 1550°F or beyond and you quench the metal, the metal could form grains.

Therefore, the best way to complete this process is by heating it to its non-metallic temperature. Then keep it in the forge at that temperature for about a minute. Then remove the steel and quench it. Certain areas of the steel might only require about 1 or 2 seconds of cooling. However, that does not mean that you have to take the steel out of the forge and quickly dip in it liquid. Do not do that! Trust me, that is a safety hazard. Think of it this way.

You take the metal out. You are in such a hurry to beat the 2-second mark that you knock off the oil to the ground. The metal drops and there is a pretty big flare. That flare catches nearby furniture or object that is flammable. Well, you know the rest.

Do not be in a hurry. The steel will hold on to some of the heat and survive for a few seconds when introduced to the air. Take it carefully and place it into the liquid for quenching. Be ready to face a small flare-up along with a high level of smoke.

# Tempering

If you have been following the instructions, then your steel should be around 65RC. At this level, it is fairly fragile so do not drop it. It might shatter upon hitting the ground.

Bring the steel to room temperature and begin tempering it once it reaches that temperature. Temper twice. Each tempering process should be done for 2 hours. Allow the steel to return to room temperature between the two processes. Ideally, your method should follow these steps: temper for 2 hours, then return to room temperature, and then back to tempering.

If you temper at 400°F, then you get a yield of 62RC.

If you temper at 500°F, then the yield is around 60RC.

If you temper at 600°F, then you get a yield of around 57RC.

You should ideally aim to get a yield of 60RC. That would be ideal for working with 1080 steel.

Finally, polish the steel as you see fit.

## Working with 1095 steel

### Heat Treatment

Once again, working with 1095 steel is pretty simple. It is a steel with high carbon content and you can use it to forge shapes easily. It does have lower traces of manganese than other steel that are part of the 10XX series (such as the 1080 steel.) However, the comparatively higher rate of carbon means that it provides more carbide that can be used for providing resistance to abrasions. However, this also means that because of the extra carbon, you might have to put in more care during the heat treatment.

### Annealing

For the annealing process, you start off by heating the metal to 1475°F. Just like with 1080 steel, you then have to cool the metal at the rate of 50°F per hour. Do not cool the metal any faster. You could also go with the suggestion to cool it overnight. You have to keep the metal inside the forge to ensure the cooling is complete.

At this point, you can perform your machining or grinding process.

### Normalizing

To normalize the steel, you have to bring the temperature of the metal to 1575°F. Once the temperature has been reached, you then soak it (or quench it) for about five minutes. After those five minutes, you then allow the metal to cool in air till it reaches room temperature.

### Heat and Quenching

For the process of quenching for 1095 steel, you should be using food grade oil. I would recommend using canola oil but any vegetable oil will do. Ensure that the metal is at around 1000°F before you introduce it to the quenching process.

### Tempering

The tempering process for 1095 steel is also fairly similar to 1080 steel. However, the difference here is that once you complete quenching, heat the steel to 500°F. Once that is done, the steel will be around 66RC. This will allow it to be fairly brittle but not too much. However, I would still not recommend that you drop it. You might not destroy it entirely but you just might cause cracks to appear on it. Once again, temper it twice for a period of 2 hours each. Make sure that you are allowing it to cool. Bring it down to room temperature before you temper it again.

## Cryo Treatment

Now, this step is not entirely necessary. However, it will improve the quality of the steel you are working with. If you like, you can completely skip this step.

If you would like to complete this step, soak the steel in temperatures ranging from -90°F to -290°F. The medium you should choose for cryo treatment should be liquid nitrogen. You need to ensure that you have introduced the metal to cryo treatment for about eight hours. For this, you can even soak the metal in liquid nitrogen overnight.

## Polish

Finally, you can add in the polish to give your project that final look.

## 15N20 Steel

## Annealing

The first step that you are going to take is the annealing process. For this you begin by introducing the steel to temperatures from 1400°F to 1450°F. At this temperature, you are making sure that so there is no change in the crystal structure.

To ensure that you are improving the steel's softness, you have to heat the metal slowly. Preferably, heat it to temperatures of about 1500°F, which is about 100°F more than the critical temperature of the metal. At such temperature, the metal enters a phase known as the transformative phase. Now, you have to soak it in liquid, preferably food grade oil, for the appropriate time. At this temperature, the crystalline structure of the steel will start to gain austenite.

Once you soak the steel at the correct temperature it is time to cool the steel. You have to ensure that you cool the metal as slowly as possible. In this case, you should cool it at a rate of 70°F per hour or less. You can even cool the metal in vermiculite. Vermiculite is a type of mineral that you can dip the metal into.

What you should be doing is cooling the metal until it reaches about 100°F below the critical temperature.

## Normalizing

When you are normalizing, you follow the very same process as annealing. However, the difference lies in the cooling process. When you are about to cool the steel, then you do not place it in an insulating environment. Rather, you take the piece and leave it in the open air to cool. This is to ensure that the cooling takes place at a much slower rate. When you cool the metal faster, you do not allow the formation of cementite.

And what exactly is cementite? Well, it is the formation of iron carbide crystals in the steel. It is created to improve the hardness of the metal.

Which is why forming cementite is an important step in the process of strengthening your steel.

## Heat and Quenching

When you are working with 15N20 steel, you can make use of vegetable or canola oil. However, when using these oils make sure that you preheat them to at least 150°F. The metal itself should be at least 900°F before you plunge it into the quenching oil.

## Tempering

For the tempering process, you have to heat the knife to a temperature of about 1400°F. This brings it to a hardness of around 60 - 65 HRC. When you reach this temperature, you might notice that the knife turns a shade of red. This is important because you are ensuring that you are tempering at the right temperature. Once you have attained the temperature, then make sure you quench the tool immediately. You can use oil for the purpose of quenching. You can even make use of food oils for the quenching process. What kind of food oils you can use are mentioned further down in this section.

### Stainless Steel

## Heat Treatment

Most of the stainless steel you are going to be using for bladesmithing harden in oil. While some steels can be quenched in preheated oil, others benefit from sub-zero quenching. Just make certain you know the type of stainless steel you are working with before you decide what kind of quenching process you would like to adopt.

For our purposes, we can treat stainless just like we would treat high-carbon steel. That way, you won't face any difficulty when you subject the metal to the hardening and tempering processes. Additionally, high carbon stainless steel is the most useful steel for blademaking.

You have to first heat the stainless steel to a bright, cherry-red color, which typically occurs around 600°F. After that, you quench it in oil. If you notice that you are not getting good results in the oil that you are using, shift the stainless steel to a lighter oil as in some cases (and for some stainless steels) a lighter oil may be necessary.

## Annealing

Most of the stainless steel that you get will be in cold-rolled condition. This means that when you subject the stainless steel to annealing, you have to do it at a temperature of 1700°F. Once you reach that temperature, then you should aim to cool it as fast as you can. However, make a note to be very careful when you are cooling the metal. Do not try to shift it from the forge to the medium really fast (as we saw earlier what could happen in such scenarios). When you are cooling it, make sure that you are doing it at 800°F. This means that you have to heat the medium to about 800°F and then dip the metal into the medium.

I would recommend using oil for the purpose of quenching.

When you quench at 800°F, you are allowing the carbon and chromium in the stainless steel to combine. This is great to improve the overall quality of the steel.

You can also use water to quench the metal, but do note that the metal might receive a certain distortion. My recommendation is to try the process on another piece of stainless steel metal (one you are not using for your blade). Check the results that appear on the blade. If you are satisfied with the distortion, then you can choose to use water. If you are not, then you are better off using oil.

Try not to cool the blade in the air. You might notice a slight discoloration on the metal. However, some people prefer to have this discoloration. If you would like to see what it looks like, try it on another piece of stainless steel.

## Normalizing

When you are working with stainless steel, you are typically aiming to improve its strength. When you have increased that strength, you do not want to lose it. Hence, for the process of normalizing, you subject the steel to temperatures of 700°F. If you subject the stainless steel to higher temperatures at this point, then you might unintentionally lower the strength it has gained so far. However, many metallurgists also recommend that normalizing is not required for stainless steel. Here is an important point to remember: if you haven't added stress to the metal, then you do not have to normalize it at all.

## Heat and Quenching

When you are using stainless steels, you are using metals that have a have high alloy content. This gives them a high degree of hardness. If you would like to achieve full hardness, then you have to air-cool the stainless steel. However, do note that you are going to receive some sort of discoloration, as we had mentioned above.

If you have to harden large sections, then I recommend that you quench the steel in oil. Steel that is hardened must be tempered immediately after bringing down its temperature to room temperature. This is done in order to prevent the steel from cracking.

Sometimes, the steel is frozen at around -165°F before it is subject to tempering. If you are using martensitic steel, then you have to ensure that you are quenching it at temperatures close to 950°F. For other stainless steel types, you can introduce the metal to the quenching liquid between 850°F and 900°F.

Some stainless steels require more heat treatments than martensitic stainless steel type. However, for the purpose of making blades, the above-mentioned process will suffice.

## Tempering

Similar to alloy steels, stainless steels are hardened using tempering. You can temper stainless steel at temperatures of 1800°F. At this temperature, you can attain a hardness between 75 - 80 HRC. Once again, you can quench them in oil once the steel has been removed from the forge. Do note that the different effects that you receive using oil, water, or air. By using the right medium, you can get the desired effect that you are looking for.

## O1 Steel

## Heat Treatment

The best part about O1 steel? It is so easy to work with it and make knives. I would recommend beginners to get into bladesmithing with O1 as well. You can easily form shapes with the O1 and once done, you can even sharpen it really easily. You can use the steel to create a nice edge that does not dull easily, even after repeated use.

However (and there is always a however), O1 steel can rust more quickly than other forms of steel. Which is why you must take care that you prevent rust from catching up.

Preventing rust from developing is not a very complicated process. Simply dry and oil the knife after each use.

Now to get started with the forging process for O1 steel. You can ideally forge the metal at temperatures of about 1800°F. You can go lower should you wish to, but ideally you should never forge below the temperature of 1500°F. After you have forged the blade, you then have to follow the below processes.

## Annealing

The annealing process used for O1 is done slowly. You need to heat up the metal slowly and uniformly to temperatures of approximately 1140°F. Once the metal reaches the temperature, take it out and soak it in oil. Make sure you soak it thoroughly. After a proper quenching treatment, you then need to cool the metal. Place the metal inside the furnace and let it cool until it reaches a temperature of 1000°F.

## Normalizing

For the process of normalizing, you are going to air cool the metal. Begin by first introducing the metal into a furnace and heat it to 1600°F. Once the metal reaches the temperature, remove it from the furnace and then introduce it to still air. That's all there is to it!

## Heat and Quenching

For O1 steel, you should utilize oil for quenching. More specifically, ensure that you are working with warm and thin quenching oil. Preheat the oil to 125°F (or as specified in the instructions) before you soak the blade in it. Once you have completed quenching the steel, you have to immediately temper the metal. The steel itself should be at least 900°F before it is dipped into the oil.

## Tempering

Now it is time to temper the metal. You need to maintain the temperature at about 400°F, which allows you to achieve a hardness between 56 - 60 HRC. At this temperature, you need to temper it for about an hour to get the results that you require. This also depends on the tool that you are going to create using this steel. Say for example that you are planning on producing a sharp tool, then your tempering process might be a little different. Cutting tools typically require more hardness. To achieve the required hardness, you might have to temper them at a temperature of 350°F for about two hours. Do note that if the sections are under two inches, then you have to temper those sections for two hours. However, if the sections are more than two inches, then you have to temper them for just an hour.

## Damascus Steel (1095 and 15N20)

This is a unique steel to work with. As we have already seen, it can produce some beautiful results. This is especially suitable if you are aiming to add a little aesthetic value to the blade. We will be looking at first heat treating the metal and then I will recommend to you the etching stage of the blade as well.

## Annealing

For the annealing process, make sure that you heat the blade slowly and evenly to 1500°F. When you reach the temperature, you might notice a dull red color forming on the blade. When you notice this color, then you have to continue heating it to about 15 - 20 minutes. If you need, you can time the process using a watch or any other device. Being accurate about the timing is key here. You do not want to overheat the metal.

If the blade gets overheated, then it might suffer cracking or warping. And that is something that we are trying to avoid.

Another method of heating is to make sure that the blade goes beyond its magnetic limit. To do this, you have to heat the metal to 1400°F. Once you have reached this temperature, you can test if the metal is ready for quenching. To do this, place a magnet near the metal. If the magnet is attracted by the metal, then you might have to heat the metal some more. If the metal does not attract the magnet, then you can begin the quenching process.

## Normalizing

Once you have completed the annealing process, you simply have to take out the blade and leave it out exposed to air.

## Heat and Quenching

For the quenching process, you can use either a light or standard quenching oil. However, using an oil quenching method is only strictly necessary for making a large blade where you might need the toughness. Otherwise, you can choose to quench the metal in brine. Quenching the metal in brine is suitable for skinnier blades as you want to ensure they have a nice holding edge. Additionally, you can use brine quenching for small blades. When you use it on smaller blades, it can make the blade harder as compared to oil. However, you need to be careful when you are quenching the blade in brine. If you cool the blade too fast, then you might cause the blade to crack. To ensure that you are quenching properly, simply preheat the brine to around 100°F before you soak the metal in it. You can make a homemade brine solution. All you have to do is dissolve salt in water until you can no longer dissolve any additional salt in the water. When you reach that point, you have a brine solution.

The blade itself can be between 850°F and 950°F before you start the quenching process.

When you are working with thin blades, then you should try to quench either its point or its spine first. This prevents the blade from cracking or warping. When you are working with thick blades, then you can quench it using the cutting edge first. This ensures that you have maximum hardness.

## Tempering

We have now reached the process of tempering. For tempering, you need to make sure that you are heating the metal in a heat treatment oven. Ideally, I recommend that you start this process as soon as you have completed quenching. When you make this transfer quick, you are ensuring there are fewer chances of cracking due to residual stresses.

One of the best ways to temper the blade is to take a block or slab of steel. Then heat up the block or slab to a temperature of around 400°F, which should give your metal a hardness between 56 - 60 HRC. Once that is done, place the knife on the steel and allow it to absorb all that heat. You should keep the knife on the steel for as long as you can maintain the heat or at least for one hour.

I would recommend heating it for a period of two hours but this depends on the block and the time you are working with. If you can achieve a one-hour duration of tempering, then that will suffice as well.

# Scrap Metal

When you are working with scrap metal, you are making use of recycled steel. Most people think that there is not a lot of heat treatment for this process. That is far from it. There is more to do for scrap metal. Let us dive into it and take a look at the process involved with scrap metal.

## Annealing

Since it is scrap metal, it is not easy to find out the temperature at which you would like to subject the metal to annealing. This is why you can use a special tactic. You can just begin at 1500°F. Once the metal reaches the temperature, you can check the results. If you are not satisfied, then try again and raise the temperature to 1550°F. In such a manner, keep increasing the temperature at 50°F increments until you get the desired result. It is alright if you end up heating it a bit more than necessary or at a higher degree than you had planned. As long as you don't melt the steel, you are doing good.

## Normalizing

You have to now take the metal into the furnace to normalize it. Preheat the furnace to a temperature of 1300°F. Once that is done, place the scrap metal in the furnace for about one or two hours. I would ideally recommend one hour so that you can check how the steel looks. If you think it requires more normalizing, then, by all means, continue to subject it to the process. However, if you feel that you have reached a satisfactory level, then you can stop the normalizing process.

## Heat and Quenching

In this process, you can take the metal and soak it in oil that is preheated to around 250°F. For scrap steel, try and use fast cooling oils. They have the desired effect and they allow you to retain the hardness of the metal. The metal itself should be around 800°F when introduced to the quenching liquid.

## Tempering

For this process, we are going to use a rather unique method. Firstly, you will need to start a fire that can heat the blade evenly. You might also need coal for this process. When you see the fire burning well, break the coal and distribute them evenly into the fire. Once that is done, place the blade on top of the fire in the center. What you are going to do first is heat the blade up as much as possible.

If you would like to know whether the fire is going well or not, just check if the coals are glowing. If they are, then you have yourself a well-lit fire. If they are not, then blast the fire, even more, to make sure that the coals are heating up.

Turn the blade over as many times as you can. This prevents any cracks from forming on the blade. When the blade is preheated, place it in the center of the fire. When the blade is preheated, put it into the center of the fire.

When the blade is in the fire, turn it over every thirty seconds. Move the coals around if required and continue heating. You should be able to see the blade glow red hot. That is an indication that your tempering process is going well. Eventually, when the steel reaches a temperature of around 600°F, you can stop the tempering process.

# Chapter 4: The Clean-up Job

Once the knife has been created, it still needs to go through a few more steps. To begin with, we are going to subject it to the final grinding process. What is that? Let me explain it to you.

## Final Grind

One of the most important steps that you are going to be taking is the final grind. In order to make this step successful, you should ensure that you are doing this process slowly and carefully.

In all honesty, there are no substantial differences between the final grind and any other grinding process. The steps are actually the same. Perhaps the minor difference lies in the amount of steel that you are planning to remove. Also, you might have to take note of the grit of the belts you are going to use. If you are confused about what I am talking about, then let me explain. When you are grinding, you essentially use belts to smoothen out the knife you created. This helps you remove any excess steel that may be present on the knife.

The main reason for using the final grind is to lower the cutting edge down to a thickness that you can sharpen with. Additionally, you also remove any coarse grit scratches. Now you might need to know how far down you need to take the edge.

My recommendation is that you take the edge down to approximately ten-thousandths of an inch for slicing of cutting tools. For a heavy-duty blade, about fifteen-thousandths. If you are making a sword, then you might need at least twenty-five thousandths of an inch.

If you have a blade and this level of thickness, then you might not have a super sharp edge. However, if you are creating a large blade like a sword (perhaps you would like to cut pineapples?), then you don't really need a sharp edge.

Once again, it all depends on the type of blade that you are aiming to make. If you want a really sharp edge, grind the blade so that you have a thinner edge. If you want a more rugged edge, then grind the blade so that it is thicker. If you would like to know what thickness your knife should be, then consider this: a carving knife has a thickness of about 0.35mm. This ensures that the knife becomes perfect for cutting. For thicker measurements, you can go anywhere from 0.36mm to 0.45mm.

After you begin to notice that the blade is fully heat-treated and tempered, you can begin the final grind. Make sure you grind the blade slowly. Cool the blade frequently. If you notice that the blade begins to change colors, you are destroying the temper. If this continues, then you might end up annealing the blade to the point where it is useless. So prevent the blade from changing colors or getting too hot.

Here is a simple tip to keep in mind. If you find the blade too hot to handle, then that means it actually is too hot. You can reduce the degree of heat that builds up by using newer and sharper belts for the final grinding.

All that you are trying to achieve in the final grading is the same results of the rough grind process. You are also cleaning up the grind lines and ensuring that all of the unnecessary hammer marks are removed. You can do some minor changes as well at this point. Do make sure that you do not overheat the steel while you are performing your change.

If you can manage to grind and polish the flat areas of the blade in advance, then make sure that you do the same for the bevels. You will find it easier to keep the grind lines sharp and clean.

## Fitting

After you have completed the final grind, you are now ready to add in the fittings. There are several ways to go about completing this process. You can make them from a sheet, bar, or even a rod of steel or other material. Or alternatively, the fittings can be filed, cast, or forged into shape. Since you are the knife maker, the final decisions are up to you. There is no easy or hard method. It is just a matter of preference.

You might also have to remember that some blades don't require a bolster or other fittings. Examples of the blades that we are talking about are boot knives and hunters.

If you are making a hidden-tang knife, then the best thing you can do is attach the grip material to the tang before you begin to work on the fitting. When you do this, you will be able to fix the grip onto the tang without softening the joint between the guard and the blade.

When you are preparing the fitting for a hidden-tang design, begin with a piece of stock that is a little wider and longer than what you want to end up with.

The guard can be brass, bronze, copper, German silver, stainless steel, or just about anything you have on hand and want to use. Just be certain that the material isn't too hard to drill through and/or file or you will not be able to achieve a good fit on the blade.

## Sharpening

Finally, we reach the sharpening stage. When you are sharpening the knife, then it means you have officially reached the last step. In this process, you are trying to put on a good edge to the blade. There are many ways that you can get a sharp edge, the method you choose is up to you.

When you are about to add the first edge on your knife, make sure that you are doing it using a machine. Any further sharpening should be done using a stone. You could also use a leather strap for this purpose.

The main thing that you should focus on is to keep the cutting edge going down the center of the blade's edge. This center portion of the edge is known as the spine of the backbone.

With that, you have completed the cleaning and finishing processes necessary for the knife.

# Chapter 5: On the Table

Heat Treatment Temperature Table

| Composition | Harden °F | Temper °F | Anneal °F | Normalize °F | Quench |
|---|---|---|---|---|---|
| Medium Alloy | 1700-1800 | 350-1000 | 1550-1600 | 0 | Air |
| High Carbon | 1800-1875 | 400-1000 | 1600-1650 | 0 | Air |
| Hot Work Alloy | 1825-1875 | 1000-1200 | 1550-1650 | 0 | Air |

## List of Welding Flux

## Arc Welding

In the process of arc welding, you are using a power supply and also electrodes in order to perform the welding process. What you are doing is creating an arc between the electrode and the material that you would like to weld. The material that you weld is probably composed of mainly metal as this method is often used in order to fuse metals together. Arc welding is one of the most popular types of welding. But are there any more types? Let us look at some, shall we?

Here is a list of arc welding options that you can use:

- Carbon Arc Welding

- Bare Metal Arc Welding

- Gas Metal Arc Welding

- Plasma Arc Welding

- Atomic Hydrogen Welding

- Shielded Metal Arc Welding/MIG Welding

# Chapter 6: Guide to Building a Simple Forge

There's one thing you have to face if you desire to work with metals—heat is needed. With the availability of heat, you can make any metal, no matter how tough, submit to your will. You'll never gain complete mastery over this stubborn material without heat. However, it isn't difficult to finally make the decision to take another step toward teaching yourself this smithing skill.

You'd learn how to build an effective but simple forge in this section. With this forge, you can heat steel hot enough to the temperature needed to effortlessly shape it.

## Step 1: Materials

Some rocks, like granite, a bucket of mud, and an iron or steel pipe, are required for building a forge. Due to the fact that heating galvanized metal is bad, do not give consideration to galvanized pipes. However, coating the pipe in some layers of mud and using the forge outside for proper ventilation can be used to counter it.

## Step 2: Construction

Place the rocks in a ring. You can create it any size you desire, but it is preferable to keep it small so as to get maximum heat.

After this, you need to use a thick layer of mud to coat the inside of the forge. Coating with mud will prevent the ground from absorbing the heat. The rocks are also insulated by the mud so they don't crack.

## Step 3: First Firing

To get the fire sufficiently hot, the metal pipe should be connected to a vacuum cleaner on blow. Some steel can be heated to test how hot it gets and then melted in the can.

## Step 4: It Gets Hot!

The forge at this point reaches forging temperatures able to melt steel.

## Step 5: Conclusion

The forge can be upgraded a bit and made bigger.

# Chapter 7: Sending Out Metals for Heat Treatment

You have to realize that heat treatment is a fairly long process. You may not be able to achieve the quality that you are looking to achieve, especially if you lack the time to practice. This is because heat treatment requires all your attention, If you believe that you are not capable of doing all the work yourself, then you have other options.

One of those options is to look for outside help.

<u>Let us look at the why's of sending your blades outside.</u>

You do not have all the time to spend on heat treatment. This is a common scenario for many beginners. Sometimes, they might find out while they are working about how much time they have. I would recommend that you try out the process by yourself. If you feel that you can handle it, then you are good to go. If you cannot, then you might have to send it outside.

In some cases, you may not be able to afford all the objects required for the process of heat treatment.

There are always emergencies that you have to attend to. But at the same time, you do not want to let go of your process.

The process might be too complex to master. This is also true for many beginners. Heat treatment is indeed a complex process and even veterans of the trade can make mistakes in their process.

<u>How do you send you blades outside for treatment?</u>

Firstly, you need to identify nearby bladesmiths. You might have to do some research in order to find someone who meets the below criteria:

- They are able to match your price requirements.

- They can produce good-quality products.

Do note that you might not necessarily be able to find a bladesmith who provides inexpensive services and gives you good results.

Here is a list of companies that you can consider for your heat treatment processes (do note that knife maker is headquartered in Canada):

http://www.buckknives.com/resources/pdf/Paul_Bos_Brochure.pdf

http://www.petersheattreat.com/cutlery.html

http://www.texasknife.com/vcom/privacy.php#services

http://www.knifemaker.ca/ (Canada)

# Chapter 8: Common Mistakes and How To Avoid Them

## Overheating

Whenever you are working with low alloy metals, you can often land yourself into a spot where you can cause overheating and burning. When you work with temperatures higher than 2200°F, then you are likely to cause the destruction of the steel or other forms of low alloy metals. In other cases, you can cause the deterioration of the properties of the metal due to poor administration of the heat treatment.

When you cause such mechanical problems due to heat treatment, then you end up affecting the treated metal's toughness and strength.

## How to Avoid Overheating

Firstly, you have to make sure that you are following the steps mentioned in this book. Try and use the temperatures mentioned here. In many cases, knife makers might feel the urge to experiment. This is okay. But you have to make sure that you are taking steps after performing thorough research.

There are also other ways you can ensure that you do not cause overheating. You can check the tools you are using to work with the metals. Ensure that these tools are of high-quality. Be certain that they are protected with anti-decarburizing solutions. If you could not heat the metal evenly, then you should allow it to cool first. Once it has cooled down, you can reheat it again to reach the right temperature.

## Using the Wrong Type of Metal

You might think that people could never mistake the type of metal that they are using but you could not be more wrong. Why do such situations occur? Sometimes, when you are stocking materials in your workshop, you can add different kinds of metals. In such cases, it is easy to get confused about the metals you have in your inventory if you don't label them.

You might actually end up using the wrong metal and that could be a disaster. Not only have you wasted material, but you have incurred a loss of time and money on your end. Getting materials is not always cheap.

## How Do You Avoid This

Make sure that you have labeled all the materials you have. Perform an inventory check regularly. Make sure that you are certain of the numbers you have. Always be certain of what you are using. Double check the material before you put it into the furnace. Most importantly, do not be in a hurry to get started. Take your time to make sure you have the right metals and tools.

## Wrong Steps

When you temper before the metal is ready for tempering, then you might create a small problem in the process. In order to ensure that you are not making any such mistakes, you have to focus on getting the steps right. In many cases, simply choosing to work with the annealing process without knowing might cause harm. You could cause cracks to form on the surface. You might be none the wiser. That might eventually impact your work.

## How to Avoid Them

Make sure that you are making note of the steps before doing them. If you prefer, look at the steps first. See if they make sense to you. If you need to research further, then make sure you do. Look out for expert advice before you start. Once you are absolutely certain of the steps, then you can begin working on the metal.

## Quality

It is okay to start off with cheap materials in the beginning. You may not want to risk using an expensive metal before you get a little practice. However, know that by using cheap materials, you might not get the results that you want. You might get an inferior quality product. You might notice cracking on the product. You might even spot some sort of discoloration. These are all expected of a material that is cheap and not sourced with higher-quality standards.

## How to Avoid Them

Right. This one is a tricky solution. You see, you might not want to invest in high-quality materials right at the beginning. However, what I recommend is for you to look at your needs. If you are practicing, then it is alright to skimp out on quality. But with that, you might not get the exact results that you are hoping to see. This might throw your observations in another direction. You might not be able to make proper evaluations. So think about it before you decide on what quality of metal you would like to invest in.

# Conclusion

Heat treatment is a satisfying process. The hard work that you put into it reaps some incredible results. Of course, it all depends on the efforts and the time you put into it.

Do go through this book carefully before you jump in on the heat treatment processes. Make sure you understand the concepts. Most importantly, be careful when you are working with metals.

Always put yourself first. Are you in a safe environment? Are you keeping yourself protected? Are you staying a safe distance from fire and other harmful objects?

Remember, there is no point in trying something when you are not feeling safe.

Another factor that you must consider is that heat treatment is a fairly time-consuming process. I have already mentioned it in Chapter 6 but it is worth mentioning once again. When you are aware of this, you might decide how best to approach the heat treatment process and whether you would like to complete it yourself or seek outside assistance.

Another thing to note is the simple pleasure that you derive out of the whole process of heat treatment. Simply watching your blade come to life is one of the most enjoyable sensations you can experience. I am sincerely hoping that you have such an exquisite feeling yourself as you work with many metals.

So keep yourself protected and enjoy a wonderful heat treatment process.

Printed in Great Britain
by Amazon

65263901R00131